# Spare Me the Details!

# Spare Me the Details!

✦

## A Short History of Western Civilization

*Sara S. Drogin*

iUniverse, Inc.
New York  Bloomington  Shanghai

# Spare Me the Details!
## A Short History of Western Civilization

iUniverse books may be ordered through booksellers or by contacting:

iUniverse
1663 Liberty Drive
Bloomington, IN 47403
www.iuniverse.com
1-800-Authors (1-800-288-4677)

ISBN: 978-0-595-47047-1 (pbk)
ISBN: 978-0-595-91329-9 (ebk)

Printed in the United States of America

For my family, of course—and for those of you who have ever said,
"I wish I knew more about history."

# Contents

Foreword. . . . . . . . . . . . . . . . . . . . . . . . . . . . . . . . . . . . . . . . . . . . . . . xiii

Preface . . . . . . . . . . . . . . . . . . . . . . . . . . . . . . . . . . . . . . . . . . . . . . . . . xv

**CHAPTER 1**  The Ancient Greeks: Founders of Western
             Civilization 2000–30 B.C. . . . . . . . . . . . . . . . . . . . . . 1

Early Greek History; the Mycenaeans, the Dark Ages (2000–1100 B.C.) . . . . . . . . 1

The Greek Renaissance: Towards a Common Culture (800–500 B.C.) . . . . . . . . . 2

Classical Greece (500–323 B.C.). . . . . . . . . . . . . . . . . . . . . . . . . . . . . . . . . . . 4

The Greeks at War (490–404 B.C.) . . . . . . . . . . . . . . . . . . . . . . . . . . . . . . . . . 6

Alexander the Great (356–323 B.C.) . . . . . . . . . . . . . . . . . . . . . . . . . . . . . . . . 7

The Hellenistic Age (323–30 B.C.). . . . . . . . . . . . . . . . . . . . . . . . . . . . . . . . . . 9

**CHAPTER 2**  The Ancient Romans: Preservers, Adapters and
             Disseminators of Western Civilization
             753 B.C.–476 A.D.. . . . . . . . . . . . . . . . . . . . . . . . . . . . 11

From Monarchy Through Republic (753–146 B.C.) . . . . . . . . . . . . . . . . . . . . . . 11

The Punic Wars (264–146 B.C.) . . . . . . . . . . . . . . . . . . . . . . . . . . . . . . . . . . . 13

The Transition to Empire; The Empire Through the Pax Romana
(146 B.C.–180 A.D.) . . . . . . . . . . . . . . . . . . . . . . . . . . . . . . . . . . . . . . . . . 14

The Roman Empire: Decline and Division; The End of the Western Roman
Empire (180–476 A.D.) . . . . . . . . . . . . . . . . . . . . . . . . . . . . . . . . . . . . . . . 17

The Rise of Christianity (4 B.C.–313 A.D.) . . . . . . . . . . . . . . . . . . . . . . . . . . . 18

**CHAPTER 3**  The Byzantines: Preservers of the Western Legacy,
             with an Eastern Twist 293 B.C.–1453 A.D. . . . . . . . 20

The Achievements of the Emperor Justinian (527–565) . . . . . . . . . . . . . . . . . . . 20

The Byzantine Empire Goes Its Own Way; Its Legacy (1054–1453) . . . . . . . . . . 21

**CHAPTER 4**  The Rise of Islam 622–1100 . . . . . . . . . . . . . . . . . . . 23

Mohammed and His Teachings (570–700) . . . . . . . . . . . . . . . . . . . . . . . . . . . . 23

The Spread of Islam; Islamic Civilization (700–1100) . . . . . . . . . . . . . . . . . . . . 25

**CHAPTER 5**     The Middle Ages 500–1350 . . . . . . . . . . . . . . . . . 27

The Early Middle Ages: Feudalism, Manorialism, the Church (500–1000) . . . . . . 27

The Art of the Period . . . . . . . . . . . . . . . . . . . . . . . . . . . . . . . . . . . . . . . . . . . . 30

Two "Lights" in the Dark: Charlemagne and Alfred the Great . . . . . . . . . . . . . . 31

Charlemagne (742–814) . . . . . . . . . . . . . . . . . . . . . . . . . . . . . . . . . . . . . . . . . . 31

Alfred the Great (849–899) . . . . . . . . . . . . . . . . . . . . . . . . . . . . . . . . . . . . . . . . 32

The High Middle Ages (1000–1350) . . . . . . . . . . . . . . . . . . . . . . . . . . . . . . . . . 34

The New Scholarship in the Age of Faith . . . . . . . . . . . . . . . . . . . . . . . . . . . . . . 34

Heavenly Architecture: the Gothic Cathedral . . . . . . . . . . . . . . . . . . . . . . . . . . . 35

Political Change in England (1066–1215) . . . . . . . . . . . . . . . . . . . . . . . . . . . . . 36

A Grim End: The Black Death . . . . . . . . . . . . . . . . . . . . . . . . . . . . . . . . . . . . . . 37

**Overview The Early Modern Era 1350–1550** . . . . . . . . . . . . . . . . . . . 38

What Do We Mean by "Early Modern"? . . . . . . . . . . . . . . . . . . . . . . . . . . . . . . . 38

**CHAPTER 6**     The Renaissance 1350–1550 . . . . . . . . . . . . . . . . . 39

The Early Italian Renaissance (1350–1450) . . . . . . . . . . . . . . . . . . . . . . . . . . . . 39

The High Renaissance in Italy (1450–1550) . . . . . . . . . . . . . . . . . . . . . . . . . . . 41

The Northern Renaissance (1450–1600) . . . . . . . . . . . . . . . . . . . . . . . . . . . . . . 43

**CHAPTER 7**     The Age of Discovery and Conquest
1350–1700 . . . . . . . . . . . . . . . . . . . . . . . . . . . . . 46

Europeans Explore the Globe . . . . . . . . . . . . . . . . . . . . . . . . . . . . . . . . . . . . . . . 46

Conquest and Colonization . . . . . . . . . . . . . . . . . . . . . . . . . . . . . . . . . . . . . . . . 47

Effects of the Age of Discovery . . . . . . . . . . . . . . . . . . . . . . . . . . . . . . . . . . . . . . 48

**CHAPTER 8**     The Reformation 1517 and Beyond . . . . . . . . . . . . 50

Background to the Reformation . . . . . . . . . . . . . . . . . . . . . . . . . . . . . . . . . . . . . 50

Martin Luther and Protestantism . . . . . . . . . . . . . . . . . . . . . . . . . . . . . . . . . . . . 51

The Reformation Spreads . . . . . . . . . . . . . . . . . . . . . . . . . . . . . . . . . . . . . . . . . . 51

Henry VIII and the English Reformation . . . . . . . . . . . . . . . . . . . . . . . . . . . . . . 52

The Catholic Church Responds . . . . . . . . . . . . . . . . . . . . . . . . . . . . . . . . . . . . . 53

**CHAPTER 9**     Major States in the Seventeenth Century . . . . . . . . . 54

The Thirty Years' War (1618–1648) . . . . . . . . . . . . . . . . . . . . . . . . . . . . . . . 55

Major European States . . . . . . . . . . . . . . . . . . . . . . . . . . . . . . . . . . . . . . . . . 55

France . . . . . . . . . . . . . . . . . . . . . . . . . . . . . . . . . . . . . . . . . . . . . . . . . . . . . . 55

England . . . . . . . . . . . . . . . . . . . . . . . . . . . . . . . . . . . . . . . . . . . . . . . . . . . . 56

The Austrian Empire . . . . . . . . . . . . . . . . . . . . . . . . . . . . . . . . . . . . . . . . . . 57

The Holy Roman Empire . . . . . . . . . . . . . . . . . . . . . . . . . . . . . . . . . . . . . . . 57

Russia . . . . . . . . . . . . . . . . . . . . . . . . . . . . . . . . . . . . . . . . . . . . . . . . . . . . . . 58

America . . . . . . . . . . . . . . . . . . . . . . . . . . . . . . . . . . . . . . . . . . . . . . . . . . . . . 59

Society in the 1600s . . . . . . . . . . . . . . . . . . . . . . . . . . . . . . . . . . . . . . . . . . . 60

Overview The Age of Revolutions 1550–1900 . . . . . . . . . . . . . . . . . . 62

Revolutions and the Modern Age . . . . . . . . . . . . . . . . . . . . . . . . . . . . . . . . . 62

CHAPTER 10    The Scientific Revolution and the Enlightenment
1550–1780 . . . . . . . . . . . . . . . . . . . . . . . . . . . . . . . . . 64

The Scientific Revolution (1550–1700) . . . . . . . . . . . . . . . . . . . . . . . . . . . . 64

Copernicus, Kepler, Galileo, and Heliocentrism . . . . . . . . . . . . . . . . . . . . . . 64

Newton and His Laws; Other Contributors to the Scientific Revolution . . . . . . . . 65

The Arts During the 1600s . . . . . . . . . . . . . . . . . . . . . . . . . . . . . . . . . . . . . . 66

The Enlightenment (1700–1780) . . . . . . . . . . . . . . . . . . . . . . . . . . . . . . . . . 67

Hobbes and Locke: Key Pre-Enlightenment Philosophers . . . . . . . . . . . . . . . . 67

The Enlightenment Flourishes in France . . . . . . . . . . . . . . . . . . . . . . . . . . . . 68

Other Important Enlightenment Thinkers . . . . . . . . . . . . . . . . . . . . . . . . . . . 69

The Enlightenment and Art . . . . . . . . . . . . . . . . . . . . . . . . . . . . . . . . . . . . . 70

Conclusion . . . . . . . . . . . . . . . . . . . . . . . . . . . . . . . . . . . . . . . . . . . . . . . . . . 70

CHAPTER 11    The American Revolution 1763–1783 . . . . . . . . . . 71

An American Identity Emerges . . . . . . . . . . . . . . . . . . . . . . . . . . . . . . . . . . . 71

Tensions with Britain . . . . . . . . . . . . . . . . . . . . . . . . . . . . . . . . . . . . . . . . . . 72

The American War of Revolution (1775–1783) . . . . . . . . . . . . . . . . . . . . . . . 73

The War's Conclusion: The United States of America . . . . . . . . . . . . . . . . . . . 74

CHAPTER 12    The French Revolution 1789–1815 . . . . . . . . . . . . 77

Causes of the French Revolution . . . . . . . . . . . . . . . . . . . . . . . . . . . . . . . . . . 77

The Early Years . . . . . . . . . . . . . . . . . . . . . . . . . . . . . . . . . . . . . . . . . . . . . . . 78

The Revolution Intensifies . . . . . . . . . . . . . . . . . . . . . . . . . . . . . . . . . . . . . . 80

Napoleon Bonaparte and the French Empire...........................81

Napoleon's Defeat and the Congress of Vienna........................82

**CHAPTER 13**   The Industrial Revolution 1760–1830...........84

Britain Industrializes...............................................84

Effects of the Industrial Revolution in Britain........................85

The Industrial Revolution Spreads..................................86

New Ideas and Movements: Marxism and Romanticism...................87

Conclusion.......................................................88

**CHAPTER 14**   The United States in the 1800s: From Revolution to Evolution..............................89

Establishing the New Government: Challenges at Home.................89

Establishing the New Government: Challenges Abroad..................91

The Lure of the West: Manifest Destiny.............................92

The Union Tested: The Civil War and Reconstruction..................93

Immigration......................................................95

Industrialization: Magnates and Workers............................96

The Evolving Women's Movement...................................97

**CHAPTER 15**   Intellectual Revolutions of the 1800s and Early 1900s..................................99

Liberalism: John Stuart Mill and Mary Wollstonecraft.................99

Socialism and Communism........................................100

The Emergence of Nationalism....................................101

The Giants: Darwin, Freud and Einstein............................101

The Arts in the Late 1800s and Early 1900s: The Beginning of Modernism ....103

**CHAPTER 16**   The Great War: World War I 1914–1918.......106

Preface to the War: Germany and Italy Become Nation States..............107

The Underlying Causes of World War I..............................108

The Age of Imperialism...........................................108

The Glorification of War..........................................109

Nationalism and International Relations.............................109

World War I: The Major Engagements...............................111

Two Major Changes in 1917:.....................................113

Revolution in Russia . . . . . . . . . . . . . . . . . . . . . . . . . . . . . . . . . . . . . . . . 113

The United States Enters the War. . . . . . . . . . . . . . . . . . . . . . . . . . . . . . . 115

The Results of the Great War . . . . . . . . . . . . . . . . . . . . . . . . . . . . . . . . . . 115

The Impact of World War I on Culture . . . . . . . . . . . . . . . . . . . . . . . . . 117

**CHAPTER 17**   The Period between the Wars; World War II
Begins 1919–1939 . . . . . . . . . . . . . . . . . . . . . . . 119

The 1920s: Italy, Germany, the U.S.S.R., and the United States. . . . . . . . . . . . . 119

Italy . . . . . . . . . . . . . . . . . . . . . . . . . . . . . . . . . . . . . . . . . . . . . . . . . . . . . 119

Germany. . . . . . . . . . . . . . . . . . . . . . . . . . . . . . . . . . . . . . . . . . . . . . . . . . 120

The U.S.S.R . . . . . . . . . . . . . . . . . . . . . . . . . . . . . . . . . . . . . . . . . . . . . . . 121

The United States . . . . . . . . . . . . . . . . . . . . . . . . . . . . . . . . . . . . . . . . . . 122

The Stock Market Crash and Great Depression . . . . . . . . . . . . . . . . . . . . 123

The 1930s: Hitler, Mussolini, Stalin, and the Start of WWII . . . . . . . . . . . . . . 123

American Isolationism and Pearl Harbor. . . . . . . . . . . . . . . . . . . . . . . . . . 126

**CHAPTER 18**   World War II 1939–1945 . . . . . . . . . . . . . . . . . . 128

The War in Europe (1939–1943) . . . . . . . . . . . . . . . . . . . . . . . . . . . . . . . 128

The War in the Pacific (1931–1945) . . . . . . . . . . . . . . . . . . . . . . . . . . . . 130

The North African Campaign. . . . . . . . . . . . . . . . . . . . . . . . . . . . . . . . . . 131

Other Aspects of World War II. . . . . . . . . . . . . . . . . . . . . . . . . . . . . . . . . 132

The Conclusion of World War II . . . . . . . . . . . . . . . . . . . . . . . . . . . . . . . 132

A World Changed by War . . . . . . . . . . . . . . . . . . . . . . . . . . . . . . . . . . . . 133

The Arts After World War II . . . . . . . . . . . . . . . . . . . . . . . . . . . . . . . . . . 136

**CHAPTER 19**   The Cold War 1945–1989 . . . . . . . . . . . . . . . . . . 137

East Confronts West: Background to the Cold War . . . . . . . . . . . . . . . . . . . . . 137

The Cold War Plays Out . . . . . . . . . . . . . . . . . . . . . . . . . . . . . . . . . . . . . 139

The End of the Cold War: Gorbachev and the Collapse of the Soviet
Empire. . . . . . . . . . . . . . . . . . . . . . . . . . . . . . . . . . . . . . . . . . . . . . . . . 142

The New Republics. . . . . . . . . . . . . . . . . . . . . . . . . . . . . . . . . . . . . . . . . 143

**CHAPTER 20**   The West Today: Some Final Thoughts . . . . . . . . 144

Bibliography . . . . . . . . . . . . . . . . . . . . . . . . . . . . . . . . . . . . . . . . . . . . . . . . 147

# Foreword

After teaching high school History for two decades, there is no one more qualified than Sara Drogin to "spare us the details" and provide a clear and concise overview of Western civilization. In her eighteen years at The Wheeler School in Providence, Rhode Island, Mrs. Drogin taught everything from Ancient History to Modernism, but the experiences that served her best in writing this book were the surveys that she taught in European and World History. Teaching high school students requires multiple characteristics: wisdom, energy, and of course, extensive knowledge of the subject matter. Perhaps most significantly, teaching high school history well requires a love for the subject matter, and Mrs. Drogin's contagious enthusiasm for history inspired her students throughout her years in the classroom. Mrs. Drogin knew exactly how to hook her students with a pithy description of ancient Sparta, a witty anecdote about Louis XIV or a gripping account of a forlorn battlefield during World War I. She infused her teaching with the latest scholarship and interpretations of historical events, yet always managed to find the appropriate balance between traditional views and important new approaches to studying and writing history.

Sara Drogin brought the same knowledge and expertise to this book as she brought to her classes. The result is an accessible overview of Western civilization, brimming with essential information, excerpts from primary sources, and important connections between past and present. *Spare Me the Details!* presents a fine balance of political, social, and cultural history; for example, in the brief discussion of responses to the Industrial Revolution in Europe, one can find an explanation of the philosophical underpinnings of communism as well as the rise of Romanticism in literature and the arts. This book satisfies the needs of a wide variety of readers: European travelers who want to refresh their memory of the history of a particular region or era, readers who want background information to better understand a novel, and those who want to avoid dry textbook chapters but yearn to deepen their understanding of the Western past. Perhaps most significantly, *Spare Me the Details!* provides all of us with a better comprehension of the world today and the central role that Western civilization has played in it. This is an ideal book.

Sophie Glenn Lau
Head of the History Department
The Wheeler School
Providence, Rhode Island

# *Preface*

Why study Western civilization?

The ideas and events emanating from the West over the past 2,000 years have had an enormous impact on the globe, extending even into the present day. Powerful ideologies such as humanism, liberalism, communism, capitalism, and imperialism have shaped much of the modern world. So, too, have events as disparate as the evolution of democracy in Ancient Greece and the Industrial Revolution, the Reformation and the two world wars of the past century.

To understand the West is to better apprehend the world of the 21$^{st}$ century.

# 1

# The Ancient Greeks: Founders of Western Civilization 2000–30 B.C.

## Early Greek History; the Mycenaeans, the Dark Ages (2000–1100 B.C.)

Why do we begin our story of Western civilization with the Ancient Greeks?

It was the Ancient Greeks who developed many of the significant ideals and practices that shaped Western civilization. Perhaps the most fundamental principle underlying Western civilization is the idea that the individual has worth—that he is capable and rational, and that his achievements in this world are significant. This idea evolved approximately 2,400 years ago in Ancient Greece, and although this notion was at times submerged for centuries, it has nonetheless resurfaced time and again, and was secured in the West, for the most part, during the late twentieth century.

The tribes of people that we call "the Greeks" appeared on the southern part of the Balkan Peninsula (roughly the area that we call Greece today) around 2000 B.C. They were never a politically united group: the mountainous terrain and lack of navigable rivers in this region prevented them from coalescing into one state. In the earliest period (2000–1100 B.C.), Greece was broken into small kingdoms; monarchs governed their lands from well-fortified palaces and they ruled with the advice and support of their nobles. As time went on, Mycenae emerged as the most powerful of these kingdoms, from whence came Agamemnon, leader of the Greek forces during the Trojan War. In fact, the culture of the period 1600–1100 B.C is generally called "Mycenaean" in acknowledgment of this kingdom's wealth and power. These early Greeks constructed their palace fortifications from cyclopean stones, rocks so huge that subsequent generations of

1

Greeks believed that Cyclopes, i.e., giants, must have built them. They wrote in a language adapted from the Minoans of Crete, with whom they traded (and probably conquered), and were master smiths, creating beautiful works in gold, silver and bronze. Skeletal remains highlight the robust quality of these Mycenaeans—strong and colorful, these people and their exploits gave rise to the essential epics of Ancient Greece, Homer's *Iliad* and *Odyssey*.

Around 1100 B.C., for reasons still debated, this civilization declined and Greece suffered from 300 years of "dark ages." One theory holds that the Dorians, a group who entered Greece around this time, conquered the Mycenaeans and eventually integrated into the peoples that we call Greek. In any event, literacy was lost and only a strong bardic tradition preserved the tales of the Mycenaean age.

## The Greek Renaissance: Towards a Common Culture (800–500 B.C.)

Around 800 B.C., Greek civilization experienced a rebirth. Over 300 city-states evolved, with Athens, Sparta, Thebes, and Corinth among the larger ones. As their populations grew, many city-states began to establish overseas colonies, most of which were located along the coast of Anatolia, in Sicily, and in southern Italy. Yet despite their division into these separate city-states, the peoples of Greece slowly began to regard themselves as a single group—Hellenes they called themselves—and as a people distinct from others. Indeed, they called foreigners *barbaroi* or "jabberers."

This sense of Hellenism emerged for several reasons. First, the Greeks shared a common spoken and written language; around 750 B.C. they had developed an alphabet, based on the Phoenician alphabet, with which to record their language. Additionally, all Greeks shared the same pantheon of gods. They believed that Zeus, king of the gods, ruled the world from Mt. Olympus along with his wife Hera; his brother Poseidon governed the seas, and his other brother, Hades, commanded the underworld. Other important deities were Athena, goddess of wisdom (for whom Athens was named), Apollo, the sun god, Hermes, the messenger god, and Minerva, goddess of the moon and the hunt. The Greeks also shared a faith in the advice of the Delphic oracle, a woman whose prophecies they believed were inspired by Apollo. The Olympics, those pan-Hellenic games first held in 776 B.C. (the date from which the Greeks began their history), also served to unite them. During the time of the Olympic games, all warfare ceased as Greek men competed for glory on the athletic fields, rather than on the battlefields. Finally, Homer's epics became the great national stories of all the Greeks and helped to forge a common culture.

Legend has it that around 750 B.C., Homer, the blind poet, gave final form to *The Iliad* and *The Odyssey*. His *Iliad* recounts the tale of the united Greek kingdoms battling against the wealthy city of Troy, located on the Hellespont (Dardanelles) in Asia Minor. The story goes that the Trojan prince Paris wooed Helen away from her Greek husband, Menelaus, king of Sparta. The Greeks determined to get Helen back and to restore their tarnished honor. Led by Agamemnon, king of Mycenae, the Greeks waged war against the Trojans for 10 years and ultimately defeated them. The great heroes of the tale are Achilles, the foremost Greek warrior, and Hector, the noble Trojan prince. *The Iliad* celebrates heroism, loyalty, and honor, and explores a person's obligations to his community. *The Iliad* also established the pantheon of gods that all Greeks would embrace. *The Odyssey* relates the adventures of the Greek hero, Odysseus, who suffered many trials over his 10-year journey home to his wife and son in Ithaca following the Trojan War. This epic emphasizes ideals of courage, determination, and cleverness—qualities necessary for Odysseus to reach his home.

So was there an actual Trojan War? Heinrich Schliemann, an amateur German archaeologist, believed that there must be truth behind the legend. Beginning in the 1870s, and using Homer's *Iliad* as his guide, he excavated at a site called Hissarlik in Turkey and discovered the remains of nine ancient cities, one built upon the next. He found a treasure trove of gold in the debris of the city at level II and believed that this must be the Troy of legend; in the view of many archaeologists today, the city at level 7A has a better claim to be the fabled city. Many historians feel that there might have been a war, or even a series of wars, in ancient times, fought for control of the Dardanelles, those key straits that allow passage from the Mediterranean to the Black Sea. (Indeed, these straits have long held strategic importance and have generated many efforts to control them, even into the twentieth century.)

During the next 300 years, from 800 to 500 B.C., one of the most significant revolutions in history transpired: the singular, human voice was given heed and recorded for posterity. Thus we have individuals like Hesiod, writing in the eighth century B.C., about practical, daily concerns in his *Works and Days*. Hesiod also helped to establish the genealogy of the Greek gods in his work, *Theogony*, adding dimension to Homer's pantheon. Sappho of Lesbos, the first woman poet whose name has come down to us, wrote her love poems to both men and women a century later. This idea—that one person's thoughts are worthy of note—is truly revolutionary.

The belief in the merit of the individual is essential to the development of democracy. And, as time went on, some of these city-states, like Athens, evolved from monarchies into direct democracies in which all the (male) citizens assembled to vote for their leaders, and on every piece of legislation. In Athens, this assembly of citizens elected the 10 *strategoi*, or generals, who advised the assembly in matters regarding war and peace, and who led the army and navy in times of war. The committee that administered city business, the *boule*, as well as the individuals selected for a jury pool, were chosen by lot. What faith this illustrates in the capabilities of each and every citizen, to believe that even when chosen by chance, he will do a creditable job! This very empowering idea—the belief in the worth of the individual—certainly helped contribute to the flowering of Classical Greek civilization, which reached its acme in Athens during the fifth and fourth centuries B.C.

Before we move on to discuss this, however, we should also note that Sparta, a major city-state, evolved in the opposite direction of Athens. Although Sparta's leaders—two kings—were indeed elected by the citizenry, the citizens ultimately served the state with no purchase given for individual expression. State elders determined whether a baby would live or die; weak infants—those who would never bear healthy children or mature into strong soldiers—were left to die of exposure. Boys were taken from their families at age seven and grew up in barracks; with no shoes, scant clothing, and meager rations, these boys were toughened into highly disciplined soldiers. They would live in the barracks, even if married, until age 30, when they were allowed to join their families. It was at 30 that men were considered citizens and had the right to vote. All the energies of the citizens were devoted to the state; indeed, a huge population of slaves, called helots, performed most of the manual labor.

Other Greeks admired the Spartans, despite their very different culture. An ancient tale has it that when an elderly man passed by rows of spectators from the various city-states, seeking a seat at some pan-Hellenic game, only the Spartans rose to offer him a seat. It was said that while all the Greeks knew what was right, only the Spartans *did* what was right!

## Classical Greece (500–323 B.C.)

During this period in Greece, and especially in Athens, individual talents flourished. Pericles (490?–429 B.C.)—a brilliant statesman and general—was elected to power in 443 B.C., and under his leadership Athens reached the apex of cultural brilliance. Under Pericles, for example, the Parthenon was constructed, a building which symbolizes the ideals of the Greeks—reason, moderation, order, and beauty. It was during this time period that Aeschylus, Sophocles, and Euripides wrote their tragedies and comedies, establishing models for generations of playwrights. Many of their plots came from the myths of heroes and gods, but their works address key moral issues, and their themes are those central to human experience. So timeless are their plays, that on most evenings it is possible to find one in performance on the Broadway or London stage.

Herodotus, "the father of history," recorded events for the first time in the West, chronicling among other things, the Persian wars. Thucydides, a younger contemporary of Herodotus, described the Peloponnesian war (although he died before it ended) and was the first historian to analyze his sources critically and with an eye towards posterity. He writes in his *History of the Peloponnesian War*, "If it [his book] be judged useful by those inquirers who desire an exact knowledge of the past as an aid to the interpretation of the future, which in the course of human things must resemble if it does not reflect it, I shall be content. In fine, I have written my work, not as an essay which is to win the applause of the moment, but as a possession for all time."[1]

During this time sculptors carved marble statues or cast them in bronze—realistic renderings, but also idealized, illustrating the beauty of the male and female form. Phidias is credited with sculpting or designing much of the statuary on the Acropolis, and Myron and Polyclitis are famed for their sculptures of athletes. You are probably familiar with Myron's, *The Discus Thrower*, for example. By the way, most of the original Greek statues no longer exist; what we admire as Greek statues are generally Roman copies of the original.

Great philosophers also emerged—Socrates, Plato, and Aristotle—posing such essential questions as "What constitutes happiness?"; "What is truth?"; and "What is the best form of government?" Interestingly enough, Socrates (469–399 B.C.) never wrote down his ideas, which were most often expressed in his conversations with others—thus the phrase "Socratic dialogue." It was his follower, Plato (427–347 B.C.), who preserved Socrates' conversations. Plato himself believed that every object is an imperfect reflection of the perfect idea behind it. *The Allegory of the Cave*, one of his better-known works, highlights this notion. Plato founded the Academy in Athens, devoted to philosophy and science, which lasted for 1,000 years after his death. Plato's most renowned pupil, Aristotle (384–322 B.C.), might be deemed the first scientist; he used observation and rea-

---

1.     John H. Finley, Jr., trans., *The Complete Writings of Thucydides: The Peloponnesian War* (New York: The Modern Library, 1951), 14–15.

son to better understand the natural world. Aristotle was also deeply interested in political philosophy. One of Aristotle's most famous students was Alexander the Great.

Finally, Hippocrates (460–377 B.C.) was one of the first individuals to approach disease in a scientific manner. Even today, physicians adhere to his creed, the Hippocratic Oath: "I will enter [houses] to help the sick, and I will abstain from all intentional wrongdoing and harm."[2]

## The Greeks at War (490–404 B.C.)

The Greek city-states were sometimes at war with foreign powers, and often with each other. The city-states united against the Persians, who twice launched attacks on Greece, invading it in both 490 B.C. and again in 480 B.C. During these wars, the Athenians commanded the Greek navy and the Spartans directed the army. It was during the first Persian incursion that the Greeks defeated King Darius and his Persians at the battle of Marathon; a messenger subsequently ran the 26 miles to Athens with the news of victory—the first "marathon." Ten years later Darius's son Xerxes marched the Persians into Greece, reached Athens and burned much of it. The Greeks, however, ultimately defeated the Persians at the naval battle of Salamis. The defeat of the Persians imbued the Greeks with a great sense of optimism and ensured that Greek culture, not Persian, would influence Western civilization.

However, Sparta and Athens ultimately went to war against each other, because Sparta, like a number of other city-states, felt that Athens was growing too powerful. As the Greek historian Thucydides wrote, "The real cause I consider to be the one which was formally most kept out of sight. The growth of the power of Athens, and the alarm which this inspired in Lacedaemon (Sparta), made war inevitable."[3]

The Peloponnesian war was fought from 431–421 B.C., and then after a short hiatus, continued from 415–404 B.C. Pericles, the leader of Athens, died of the plague in 429 B.C. while the city was under siege. Oddly enough, much of the genius of Athens was realized during this crucible of war. The Spartans vanquished the Athenians in 404 B.C., but fighting continued among the city-states

2.   Marvin Perry, Joseph R. Peden and Theodore H. Von Laue, *Sources of the Western Tradition*, 2nd edition, vol. I (Boston: Houghton Mifflin, 1991), 56.
3.   Helen Howe and Robert T. Howe, *Ancient and Medieval Worlds* (White Plains, N.Y.: Longman, 1987), 166.

for the next 80 years until the arrival of Philip of Macedon and his son, Alexander the Great.

Finally, we should address the role of women in Ancient Greece. Although we know that women were essential to running the household and to maintaining the fabric of society, they were not considered equals to men. (Indeed, for many Greeks, men were natural partners or lovers for each other since they could best appreciate the manly virtues.) A respectable Greek woman seldom ventured into the marketplace nor did she dine with her husband and his friends. She was not a citizen and had limited property rights. We will see that this attitude toward women prevailed, to a greater or lesser degree, through much of the history of the West. Hence the choice of the male pronoun in this text has been a conscious decision, reflecting the reality of the past.

## Alexander the Great (356–323 B.C.)

Alexander the Great left an indelible mark on history, and even today, in parts of Asia, bards recount the exploits of "Iskander," founder of cities. Born in Macedonia (a region in northern Greece) in 356 B.C., Alexander was the product of a brilliant king and military leader, King Philip of Macedon, and his wife Olympias, a fiery woman drawn to mystical religions. Alexander inherited his father's military genius, and indeed, at a young age, felt competitive with his father. When told of his father's conquests, Alexander reputedly was upset that his father would leave nothing for him to accomplish! Courageous even as a youth, Alexander was the only person in his father's court able to tame a fierce wild horse. He subdued the steed, dubbed it Bucephalus, rode it for years, and loved it greatly. When King Philip was assassinated in 336 B.C., Alexander ascended the throne; he was determined to maintain leadership over the Greek city-states—a process started by his father—and then to conquer the Persians. The Persians possessed the largest empire at the time and had continued to menace Greece. Alexander did subdue Greece and then, in 334 B.C., he left for Asia Minor with his well-trained army. He would never return to his homeland.

During the long years of conquest, Alexander carried a copy of *The Iliad* with him, annotated by his teacher Aristotle. After crossing the Hellespont, one of his first actions was to stop at ancient Troy to visit the tomb of the great Greek hero Achilles, whom Alexander claimed as an ancestor. Legend has it that Alexander exchanged a piece of his armor for some of Achilles'. Alexander's act of homage underscores his romantic nature, as well as the importance of Homer's epic to Greeks, even those living almost 1,000 years after the Trojan War. From Troy,

Alexander marched through the Middle East to Egypt, which he liberated from the Persians, and where he founded the great city of Alexandria, the first of many cities that would bear his name. From Egypt he led his troops through what is today northern Iraq, finally vanquishing the king of Persia and inheriting his vast lands. He then turned his attention to India, and in 326 B.C. began a long campaign over the treacherous Hindu Kush Mountains and across the Indus River. At this point his soldiers threatened rebellion: many had been fighting for years and were exhausted and homesick. Alexander reluctantly turned back, leading some of his army through the harsh desert of Gedrosia, where many perished. Alexander himself died in 323 B.C., age 32, in the ancient city of Babylon; the cause of his death is unknown. He had traveled 20,000 miles over the years, establishing many cities, opening up new trade routes, and conquering most of the known world.

Alexander was a brilliant general and conqueror. During difficult times, he knew how to reinvigorate and inspire his troops. As he vanquished foreign lands, he often worked with the local leaders, leaving them in place rather than incarcerating or killing them. Quite practically, there were not enough Greeks to leave behind to govern the newly acquired territories. Over time, he assumed some of the dress and practices of the Persians, to the dismay of many of his Greek troops; however, this demonstrated to the Persians his respect for their culture. Indeed, before he died he held a mass wedding in which 80 of his men were united with Persian women; he also replaced 30,000 of his Greek soldiers with Persians.

However, Alexander established no permanent central government for his empire, nor did he designate his successor. As a result, for 25 years after his death his leading generals contended for his lands. Ultimately, his empire was divided into thirds. Ptolemy, the governor of Egypt, secured control of this territory, which extended into Palestine; he established the Ptolemaic line, of which Cleopatra was the last. Seleucus, the governor of Babylon, gained control of much of the former Persian Empire and founded the Seleucid dynasty. Antigonus, a Greek general, controlled Macedonia and Greece and established the Antigonid dynasty.

Perhaps Alexander did have a vision of a cohesive empire but died too young to realize it; thus, we must acknowledge him as a great conqueror, but not an empire builder.

# The Hellenistic Age (323–30 B.C.)

Perhaps the most significant aspect of Alexander's conquests was that they spread Greek culture to other parts of the known world and exposed the Greeks to Persian and other Eastern influences. The fusion of these civilizations led to another culturally and economically rich era called the Hellenistic Age. During this period the Egyptian city of Alexandria became the center of the Hellenistic world. The Ptolemies established a center of learning, essentially a university, and constructed the most important library of the ancient West. By the first century A.D. this library contained approximately 700,000 papyrus scrolls! Trade flourished during this time; improved harbors, uniform weights and measures, and standard banking practices allowed for the flow of goods throughout the Mediterranean world.

During this fertile period mathematicians such as Euclid and Archimedes made their great contributions to the world, Euclid in the realm of plane and solid geometry, and Archimedes in geometry as well as in theoretical and applied mechanics. It was Archimedes who invented the water screw, a device which could raise water from the Nile for irrigation purposes, and which could pump water from mines and the holds of ships. He also devised the catapult, and was the first to understand the laws governing pulleys and levers. You might have heard his famous phrase, "Give me a lever and a place to stand on and I will move the earth," in reference to the lever's capacity to move objects much greater than itself.

In the Hellenistic Age new schools of philosophy developed: Stoicism stressed that people must strive to live in harmony with universal laws, and that hardship must be borne calmly; Epicureanism promoted the idea of a mind at peace and the fulfillment of wants as leading to happiness; and Cynicism taught that happiness could be realized only through achieving self-sufficiency. Diogenes, the leading proponent of Cynicism, attempted to live a simple life, which many people likened to that of a dog. In fact, the term "cynic" derives from the Greek word for "dog." You might have heard the story of Diogenes wandering the streets of Corinth with a lamp, seeking an honest man—perhaps to illustrate that there are no honest men.

Finally, some of the Western world's best-known sculptures were created during this era: the *Venus de Milo* and *Winged Victory of Samothrace*. There is a sense of drama and movement in many Hellenistic pieces that goes beyond the more controlled sculpture of Classical times. Artists also began to create works emphasizing individual features rather than idealizing their subjects.

But even as the Greek legacy continued to dominate the Mediterranean world, across the Adriatic Sea on the Italian peninsula, the city of Rome was emerging as a rival power.

# 2

# *The Ancient Romans: Preservers, Adapters and Disseminators of Western Civilization 753 B.C.–476 A.D.*

## From Monarchy Through Republic (753–146 B.C.)

The Ancient Greeks have sometimes been regarded as artists and thinkers, and the Romans as pragmatists and doers. Although this is a generalization, there is some merit to the idea. The Romans, a very practical people, freely adopted and adapted ideas and practices from other cultures. For example, they borrowed the idea of the arch from the Etruscans, neighboring Italian peoples. The use of the arch allowed the Romans to construct strong and massive structures, many of which have survived for 2,000 years. The Romans also adopted many of the Greek gods, giving them Latin names, and they emulated Greek art, copying and thus preserving many Greek masterpieces; in fact, it is fair to state that they admired all things Greek. As Rome slowly grew from a city to an empire, the Romans also devised pragmatic, efficient, and innovative ways of governing their vast holdings, ruling in such a way that people in far-flung parts of the empire were proud to say, "I am a citizen of Rome."

The traditional date for the founding of Rome is 753 B.C.; legend has it that twins named Romulus (thus Rome) and Remus, nursed by a she-wolf as infants, were the founders of Rome. Initially the Romans were a small tribe amongst many on the Italian peninsula, and Rome but an insignificant village that continued to grow over the years. During its early years, Rome evolved from a monarchy into a republic, a form of democracy in which men vote for representatives to govern them (just as in most Western nations today). Many struggles ensued on the road to creating this form of government since the patricians—the wealthier,

11

older and more established families—resisted sharing power with the plebeians, the common folk. Gradually the plebeians won more rights, and by 287 B.C. Rome was fully a republic. People voted by assembly, and each assembly had different voting responsibilities. For example, the assembly of soldiers, the *Comitia Centuriata*, elected the two consuls who led the government for a one-year tenure. In times of crisis, a dictator was chosen to lead the republic for a six-month period. The assembly of the common people, the *Concilium Plebis*, elected the tribunes, at first two, then later ten. These tribunes had the right to veto any decision of the consuls or Senate—a true safeguard for the people of Rome. The influential Senate, comprised of seasoned elders, offered advice, administered the laws issued by the consuls, ratified treaties, and received foreign dignitaries. At times in Rome's history, the Senate, in effect, governed the empire. Indeed, the motto of Rome highlights its significance: S.P.Q.R., "The Senate and the People of Rome."

In the early years, the backbone of the republic was the citizen-farmer-soldier, the independent man who tended to his fields, but also answered the call to arms when needed. Cincinnatus, a small farmer, became the symbol of the model republican citizen. In approximately 458 B.C. he was appointed dictator for six months when Rome was under attack from the Aequians, a neighboring tribe. He set aside his plow, led the Roman army to vanquish the Aequians, and returned to his fields—all within 16 days. Cincinnatus was not motivated by the quest for personal power but rather by the desire to serve his city. Subsequent generations of Romans would herald this lack of personal ambition coupled with the desire to aid the republic.

It is worth noting that a man had to be a property owner to fight for Rome, for who would strive harder than someone who had a stake in the fight? Additionally, only property owners could afford to outfit themselves with sword and armor. The virtues of these hardworking, patriotic farmers gave rise to key republican values: *pietas*—respect for authority and tradition; *fide*—being true to one's responsibilities; *in religio*—adhering to the common beliefs; and *gravitas*—that serious quality that a mature male was expected to possess. Unfortunately, these values diminished in importance over time as Rome gained in power and wealth.

And what of women? Just as in Greece, women were considered subordinate to men and could not vote or hold public office. However, they did have some property rights as well as more freedom to move about the city. In fact, in 195 B.C. a group of Roman women successfully pressured the Senate to abrogate a law that it had passed twenty years earlier restricting women's dress. Indeed, many Roman women had considerable influence as the "power behind the throne."

# The Punic Wars (264–146 B.C.)

In addition to the internal struggles between patrician and plebeian, Rome also engaged in a series of wars during this time period, at first against local tribes, then later against Carthage, the great Mediterranean power of the third century B.C. Some of these early wars were in response to attacks from neighboring tribes, but often they were preemptive. By 275 B.C. Rome had subdued most of the Italian peninsula and could draw on the strength of its allied peoples there. This large population base allowed Rome to turn its attention to Carthage, the wealthy and powerful city in North Africa that held sway over the Mediterranean. If Rome were to truly become a power, then it must vanquish Carthage—and, in a series of three wars, called the Punic Wars, Rome did destroy Carthage, but at great cost.

At the outset of the first war in 264 B.C., Roman leaders recognized that they would need a strong navy, in addition to their fine army, to defeat Carthage. In a classic example of Roman ingenuity and adaptation, they copied the design of a wrecked Carthaginian warship, but added a huge spike, lashed to the mast, which could be lowered during battle to connect two combatant ships. The idea was to "invade" the enemy ship, thereby bringing Roman expertise in fighting on land to the high seas. During the First Punic War (264–241 B.C.) Rome ultimately prevailed, seizing Sicily from Carthage and making it the first Roman province. The Second Punic War (219–202 B.C.), initiated by the Carthaginians, was carried into Roman lands by the brilliant general Hannibal. Departing from his base in Spain, Hannibal took many months to reach Italy. The most treacherous part of the journey was crossing the Pyrenees and the Alps with 40,000 soldiers, 8,000 horses and 37 elephants. After the difficult passage, only half the men and but a few elephants remained. Even with his diminished forces, this valiant leader defeated the Romans in two major battles and continued to harry them for years, destroying much Roman farmland. He received no reinforcements during this time from the leaders in Carthage—they were busy sending troops to other areas under Roman siege. As you might imagine, one of Hannibal's major challenges was keeping his army together throughout the long years in Italy. A Greek historian, Polybias, wrote this assessment of Hannibal: "Who can help admiring this man's skillful generalship, his courage, his ability, if he will consider the span of time during which he displayed these qualities? ... For 16 years on end he maintained the war with Rome in Italy without once releasing his army from service in the field; he kept vast numbers under control like a good pilot, without any sign of dissatisfaction towards himself or friction amongst themselves...."[1]

Ultimately, when the Roman general Scipio Africanus brought the war to North Africa, Hannibal was ordered home to protect Carthage. The Roman army eventually defeated the Carthaginians at the Battle of Zama in 202 B.C. As a result, Carthage was allowed to keep only its original holdings in Africa—there would be no more overseas empire—and it had to pay Rome a large war indemnity.

And what of Hannibal? This valiant leader became the head of Carthage and from this position enacted legislation to ameliorate conditions for the poor and to promote international trade. However, his actions alienated some powerful Carthaginians; additionally, influential Romans believed that he posed a continued threat so long as he lived. He ultimately had to flee Carthage, pursued by Romans, and took his life in 183 B.C. when he was 64.

The Third Punic War (149–146 B.C.) resulted from the strong anti-Carthaginian sentiment that persisted in Rome over the years, which was reinforced by the diatribes of Cato the Censor. Every speech Cato delivered to the Senate concluded with the words, "Carthage must be destroyed." Finally, on a rather spurious pretext, the Romans besieged Carthage for three years. When the starving Carthaginians surrendered, the Romans burned their city to the ground. The magnanimity that Romans had often shown their enemies disappeared in the ashes of Carthage; from it rose a new era in the history of Rome—the true beginning of its role as master of the ancient world.

## The Transition to Empire; The Empire Through the *Pax Romana* (146 B.C.–180 A.D.)

Even while fighting Carthage, Rome had engaged in campaigns against Macedonia and Greece. In subsequent years it continued its aggressive path: Roman armies traveled to Spain, Gaul, and Britain; to Asia Minor; to Africa and the Middle East. As its holdings increased, Rome demonstrated what the Roman poet Virgil deemed its "great arts": it ruled its empire efficiently and effectively with an established body of laws. With the consuls—and later an emperor—at its apex, a hierarchy of provincial governors and client kings established order and carried out Rome's will.

---

1.    Howe and Howe, *Ancient and Medieval Worlds*, 219.

Rome united its empire in a myriad of ways. It was generally lenient towards conquered peoples, as long as they swore allegiance to the emperor and to Rome. Additionally, Rome extended citizenship—with its blessing of Roman law—to the allied tribes within Italy in 88 B.C., and later to many of the conquered peoples. It also constructed extensive road systems throughout its territories to ensure the rapid travel of armies, goods, and communications. It established standardized weights and measures to facilitate commerce, and Rome's language, Latin, became the universal tongue of Empire. Rome also constructed many cities throughout Europe, replete with its hallmarks—baths, theaters, coliseums—as well as aqueducts to supply fresh water. Throughout the Mediterranean world we still find ruins of ancient Rome, enduring testaments to its power.

As time went on, however, the fabric of Roman society changed. When many of the small farmers—the traditional backbone of Roman society—returned from the Punic wars, they found that they could no longer make a living from their small landholdings. The owners of huge estates had increasingly used slaves, often prisoners of war, to work their land and were therefore producing farm goods very cheaply, more cheaply than small farmers could. Additionally, during the years of war, Rome had started to import grain from colonies such as Sicily and Sardinia, and the small farmers, once again, could not compete with this influx of inexpensive grain. They were forced to relinquish their farms, and large numbers of these unemployed farmers flocked to cities in search of jobs, where, too often, slave labor made it impossible for them to find work. Additionally, as these men lost their land, they were no longer eligible to serve in the army, an army that was needed even more as Rome extended its holdings. And as wealth poured into the city—the spoils of war, profits from increased trade—the upper classes enjoyed lives of luxury and hedonism, lives far removed from the simple virtues of the early Republic.

In subsequent years some reformers arose—the Gracchi brothers, and the generals Marius and Sulla—all of whom attempted to remedy Rome's problems. Beginning in 133 B.C., the tribune Tiberius Gracchus implemented an agrarian reform policy to redistribute land to the unemployed and impoverished masses; his brother Gaius developed overseas colonies to further carry out this policy. Both Tiberius and Gaius, hoping to help the poorer classes, sold them cheap, government-subsidized grain. In carrying out their policies, however, they challenged the power of the Senate and undermined some republican traditions. Around 100 B.C. a general named Marius developed a professional army, answering Rome's need for a larger army and providing the unemployed with jobs, although sometimes it was the general, rather than Rome, whom the army served. Sulla, another general, marched on Rome with his army in 82 B.C. and established himself as dictator for three years; he murdered his opponents and made reforms to improve the conditions of the poor. Ironically, he attempted to restore some republican traditions that he and the others had undermined in previous years! When he stepped down in 79 B.C., two of his officers, Pompey and Crassus, gained influence by dealing effectively with some military issues, one of which was a major slave revolt led by the gladiator Spartacus. However, despite some positive efforts to deal with Rome's socioeconomic problems, these individuals had, in essence, irreparably damaged the republic.

All of these challenges to the republic paved the way for Julius Caesar, the outstanding general whose *Commentaries on the Gallic War* had let the Romans know just how magnificent he was. Born in 100 B.C., Caesar was of high birth and had served Rome in various capacities. In his younger years he had spent much of his wealth subsidizing entertainments for the people of Rome, thus currying their favor. In 60 B.C. he formed an alliance (a "Triumvirate") with the powerful Pompey and Crassus, which they later renewed, to further each of their political ambitions. Caesar's successful campaign in Gaul (France), which began in 58 B.C., brought him acclaim at home and won him the loyalty of his army. However, he ultimately went to war against Pompey for control of Rome. In 49 B.C. he crossed the Rubicon River with his army in defiance of Roman law, which stated that a general could not bring his army beyond this river. He reputedly stated "The die is cast" as he crossed the Rubicon: there was no turning back. He fought Pompey, chasing him into Greece, and later Egypt, where Pompey was assassinated in 48 B.C. Caesar remained in Egypt for a year, consolidating Roman power there and placing Cleopatra, with whom he became enamored, on the throne of Egypt.

Once back in Rome, in 46 B.C., Caesar began a series of reforms: a revised and more accurate calendar (which has lasted with only slight changes to the present day); construction projects such as new roads and a new Forum; some debt relief to the poor; and an improved system of tax collection for the empire. He also hoped to reconcile his former enemies by treating them generously, often giving them positions of power. His ambition, however, was too manifest. In 44 B.C. a cabal of senators, among them his friend Brutus, assassinated him, justifying their actions by claiming to save the republic from tyranny. Rome was plunged into civil war for several years. The pro-Caesar forces, led by Caesar's adopted great-nephew Octavian, and by Caesar's friend, Marc Antony, vanquished the assassins—then ultimately turned against each other. Octavian finally defeated Antony and his love, Cleopatra; Antony died in Egypt, in Cleopatra's arms, in 31 B.C.

Octavian was the new master of Rome and its empire. He governed successfully for 43 years, and was eventually awarded the title "Augustus," the highest one. How was it that he succeeded in consolidating personal power, whereas Caesar had failed? Romans were tired of wars and most were willing to accept a strong ruler if he ensured order and stability—which Augustus did. In fact, Augustus ushered in 200 years of peace, a period called the *Pax Romana* (29 B.C.–180 A.D.)—a glorious time in the ancient world. Augustus was also very circumspect about accepting some of the honors that were offered him: he had learned well the risks of appearing too ambitious. Additionally, Augustus promoted the traditional values of the republic—simplicity in one's daily life, devotion to family, and attention to religious duties. In sum, he ruled brilliantly: he developed a better taxation system, he created an efficient bureaucracy to manage the empire, and he established his position as supreme while still seeming to respect the institutions of the republic.

# The Roman Empire: Decline and Division; The End of the Western Roman Empire (180–476 A.D.)

After his death, Augustus' successors overtly sought power, truly becoming emperors, leaders of Empire. Some of them ruled wisely—Trajan and Hadrian, for example—while some were inept and cruel, like Caligula and Nero. However, because Rome did not have a clear process for succession, power struggles and assassinations occurred frequently. From 235 to 285 A.D., for example, 26 different emperors assumed power and only one died of natural causes! As you can imagine, this instability in leadership created enormous problems. The emperor Diocletian, who governed from 285–305 A.D., attempted to resolve this issue by creating a system for succession: the emperor would choose a capable successor, called a *Caesar*, whom all would acknowledge as the heir to the throne.

Besides succession struggles, Rome was beset by many other issues starting in the third century. There were economic problems, such as the recurrent plagues that swept over Rome and killed thousands of workers; this led to a shortage of goods and then to inflation. The Roman upper classes continued to import luxury items from the East while Rome itself produced mundane, non-marketable items such as pottery and textiles; imports therefore greatly outweighed exports, and money flowed away from the Empire. Furthermore, Germanic and Asian tribes—Vandals, Ostrogoths, Huns—swept over Europe in the fourth and fifth centuries, making destructive incursions into the Empire and damaging raids on the Roman fleet. Thus Rome was pushed to its limit.

In 293 A.D. the emperor Diocletian attempted to deal with some of these problems by dividing the unwieldy empire into two halves, the Western and the Eastern halves. In the early 300s, the emperor Constantine established the capital for the East in the city of Byzantium beside the Bosporus, which he named Constantinople (called Istanbul today). This Eastern Roman Empire—eventually called the Byzantine Empire—would continue to flourish for approximately 1,000 years after the fall of the Western Roman Empire. We will discuss this more fully in Chapter III.

The Western Roman Empire ultimately succumbed to various barbarian raids. In 410 A.D. Alaric and his Visigoths pushed into the city of Rome and "vandalized" it. In 476 A.D., the traditional date for the fall of Rome, an Ostrogoth named Odoacer seized the throne of Rome from the last Western Roman emperor—and Rome's decline was complete.

Rome's achievements, however, were preserved in the Eastern Empire and, more tenuously, in the West. Rome's system of laws would eventually influence most legal systems of the West. Its efficiency in governing an empire provided a model for the Christian Church and others, and its engineering feats—aqueducts, coliseums and roads—would prove inspirational and useful for peoples of the future. Rome's reverence for Greek learning and art saved these achievements for posterity. Latin continued as the universal language of educated people throughout the Middle Ages and is the basis for modern Romance languages—Portuguese, Spanish, French, Romanian and Italian. (Although Latin-based words constitute approximately 60 percent of English, it is considered a Germanic language.) Finally, Christianity, which Constantine legalized in 313 A.D., became a major legacy of Rome.

# The Rise of Christianity (4 B.C.–313 A.D.)

In approximately 4 B.C.—during the time of Augustus' rule—a child named Jesus was born in Roman-held Palestine, in the town of Nazareth. Born and raised a Jew, when he was thirty years old Jesus began actively preaching a revolutionary message: that salvation is possible for everyone, no matter how lowly his status; that "the meek shall inherit the earth"; that God is a loving God offering forgiveness to anyone who truly repents. He enjoined people to "love thy neighbor as thyself" and to "turn the other cheek." His God was the God of the Jews, and the Old Testament prophets and patriarchs were central to his teaching. Over a period of three years he gained enough followers that Pontius Pilate, the Roman governor of Judea, perceived him as a threat and had him executed. According to his followers, Jesus rose from the dead after three days, as he had promised them he would. News of his resurrection confirmed to many, and convinced others, that he was indeed the Messiah, or Savior.

Early Christians met with much persecution—they refused to worship the Roman emperor as a god, among other things—and many were martyred for their beliefs. Their heroism in the face of death, and the appeal of Jesus' message, slowly contributed to the growth of this new religion. Around 50 years after Jesus' death, early Christians Matthew, Mark and Luke recorded stories about his life and teachings, and twenty years later, John added to these. Their accounts, called the Gospels or "Good News," form the first four chapters of the New Testament. We should note that the Gospels are not eyewitness accounts since these four individuals lived a full generation or more after Jesus.

Paul, originally called Saul, was of major importance in establishing Christianity, and his significance cannot be overstated. Paul became a convert to Christianity after Jesus' death. He energetically traveled the excellent Roman road system through Asia Minor and into Greece, establishing churches along the way. He kept in touch with these fledgling churches through letters—the New Testament contains many chapters of Paul's letters—and he helped clarify and codify early Christian belief. Paul also allowed Gentiles, i.e. non-Jews, to convert to Christianity without becoming Jews first, a practice that greatly contributed to Christianity's growth. Although we do not know when Paul was born, he died around 65 A.D.

Finally, in 313 A.D., the Roman emperor Constantine issued the Edict of Milan, which allowed the practice of Christianity. From this point onward, the Church grew and became the most important institution of the next 1,200 years.

The early Christian Church modeled itself, to some degree, on the hierarchy of the Roman government. As time went on, the head of the Church was called the pontiff, or pope; serving under him were the archbishops whose domains were called provinces; their underlings were bishops, who ran the dioceses; at the lowest, local level were the priests, who ran the parishes. As we shall see, the Church became the central, unifying force during the Middle Ages in Europe and its influence and power were profound.

# 3

# The Byzantines:
# Preservers of the Western Legacy,
# with an Eastern Twist
# 293 B.C.–1453 A.D.

Centered in its thriving and beautiful capital of Constantinople, the Byzantine Empire preserved the legacy of Rome and Ancient Greece, while eventually adding its own "Eastern" twist. The emperor Constantine chose the town of Byzantium as his capital, changing its name to Constantinople. The city was a brilliant choice, for it controlled the Bosporus, it was relatively easy to defend, and it provided ready access to both Asia and Europe. Constantinople eventually grew into a wealthy and fabulous city, replete with palaces and cathedrals, universities and monasteries, and an abundance of goods from both East and West. It is estimated that 500,000 people lived in this thriving city at its apex.

## The Achievements of the Emperor Justinian
## (527–565)

Perhaps the most notable Byzantine emperor was Justinian, who ruled from 527–565. Justinian's motto was "One empire, one church, one law," and he energetically sought to fulfill these words. His outstanding general Belisarius won multiple victories that resulted in a reunification of the Eastern and Western halves of the Roman Empire ("one empire"). However, the financial cost of these wars was enormous, and reunification, brief. Justinian also mandated that a citizen of the empire must be Christian ("one church") in an effort to bind together the great diversity of peoples. He placed himself at the head of the church and made key decisions and appointments, thus bringing the church under state control. Justinian ordered the organization and codification of Roman laws, and this great work, the *Corpus Juris Civilis,* provided a standardized law code for the empire ("one law"). These laws would prove highly influential in law codes of the West long after the demise of the Byzantine Empire. Indeed, some scholars contend that only the Bible surpasses the *Corpus Juris Civilis* in terms of its impact on Western civilization!

Many of the laws seem "modern," and their effect on our laws is clear. Consider these:

- It is better to permit the crime of a guilty person to go unpunished than to condemn one who is innocent.

- Proof is incumbent upon the party who affirms a fact, not upon him who denies it.

- In inflicting penalties, the age and experience of the guilty party must always be taken into account.[1]

Although the code did permit torture, it limited its practice.

# The Byzantine Empire Goes Its Own Way; Its Legacy (1054–1453)

Over time the Byzantine Empire diverged from the West in its language—Greek supplanted Latin in the Eastern Roman Empire—and in its architecture and art. In the West, for example, the typical cathedral was constructed in the shape of a cross, but in the East, the cathedral assumed the shape of cross with four equal arms. The interiors of these cathedrals glittered with innumerable gold tesserae and with mosaics depicting the holy family, saints and emperors. People were portrayed in a stylized manner—tall, slender and flat, with small feet and large, staring eyes. Although there was little individualization in these portrayals, they did project a sense of timelessness and dignity. St. Mark's cathedral in Venice is an excellent example of Byzantine architecture and art.

Perhaps the greatest divergence of all occurred in 1054, with the Great Schism in the Church. For centuries, Church authorities in East and West had squabbled over the use of icons, the wording of the Nicene Creed, and who should be the head of the Church: the pope in Rome or the patriarch in Constantinople.

---

1.    Perry, Peden and von Laue, *Sources,* I: 163.

Finally, in 1054, the Roman Catholic Church and the Eastern Orthodox Church, as they came to be called, broke with each other. For centuries following the schism, the Catholic Church, headed by the pope, conducted its services in Latin whereas the Orthodox Church, led by the patriarch, encouraged services in the vernacular. Thus many branches of the Orthodox Church emerged, such as the Russian Orthodox Church and the Armenian Orthodox Church.

Throughout its thousand-year history the Byzantine Empire was buffeted by attacks from invaders and by uprisings within its borders. In the eleventh century the Muslim Seljuk Turks captured some eastern provinces, and in the early thirteenth century, members of the Fourth Crusade marauded through Constantinople for three days, killing and looting. The crusaders had been encouraged in these activities by Venetian merchants who wanted to eliminate Constantinople as a trade rival—so much for the brotherhood of Christians! In 1453, the Muslim Ottoman Turks besieged and conquered the great city of Constantinople and made it the capital of their vast Ottoman empire. We will learn more about the Muslims in the next chapter.

In the big picture the Byzantine Empire preserved the scholarship of Ancient Greece and Rome and developed its own rich culture. From the magnificent Cathedral of St. Mark's in Venice, to the onion-shaped domes of the Kremlin, we can see the reach of its influence. Additionally, Greek-speaking monks traveled into the Balkans and Russia, spreading Christianity and developing the Cyrillic alphabet. (This alphabet, which adapted Slavic sounds to the Greek alphabet, is still used today.) Finally, the Byzantine Empire provided a bulwark against many invaders from the East, which allowed the fledgling Western European states to develop.

# 4

# *The Rise of Islam*
# *622–1100*

## Mohammed and His Teachings (570–700)

We now turn our attention from Europe to the Middle East, and specifically to the Arabian Peninsula. It was here in the city of Mecca that Mohammed was born in the sixth century A.D.—Mohammed, founder of Islam and father of the great Islamic civilization. This sophisticated civilization would ultimately stretch across North Africa into Spain, and across the East into India.

Topographically, the Arabian Peninsula in 600 A.D. was much as it is today—largely desert. There were a few cities along the coast, which were part of a network of trade routes leading to the north. The peoples inhabiting the vast desert were called Bedouins, nomads who were fiercely loyal to their tribe and tribal gods, but often merciless to others. Blood feuds were common between tribes, punishments severe, and widows and orphans were often treated harshly.

At this time the city of Mecca was of central importance to Bedouins and city-dwellers alike, for there, in a cube-shaped building called the *Kaaba*, was the Black Stone. All tribes believed that Allah, one of the most powerful of their many gods, had sent this stone to earth. Surrounding the *Kaaba* were idols of the other gods, making Mecca a holy city, a city of pilgrimage for the Arabian peoples.

Mohammed was born in Mecca in 570 A.D. Orphaned young, he was raised by relatives and at an early age became a camel-driver, leading caravans along the edge of the Arabian Peninsula up into Palestine and Syria. Here he came into contact with Jews and Christians with their monotheistic beliefs and their patriarchs and prophets—Abraham, Moses, and Jesus, for example. He eventually married Khadija, an older, very wealthy woman, and gave himself over to meditation. Muslims hold that while Mohammed was meditating, the angel Gabriel appeared to him, proclaiming that Mohammed was a prophet of Allah. Mohammed then began to preach a revolutionary message to the polytheistic Arabs: that there was only one God, Allah, and that each person must submit to Allah's will. (In fact, *Islam* means "submission" and a *Muslim* is "one who submits.") Allah was the single God, the God of the Jews, the Christians and the Arabs, too; Jewish and Christian patriarchs and prophets, including Jesus, became important figures in Islam, paving the way, as it were, for Mohammed, the final prophet. In his teachings Mohammed also outlawed blood feuds and encouraged kinder treatment toward orphans and women. Indeed, Mohammed restricted the number of wives that a man might have to four, and added the proviso that each wife must be treated equally. Additionally, he forbade gambling and the use of alcohol. Finally, Mohammed promised that paradise awaited the true believer, a paradise that was fertile and green, and filled with flowing fountains. (This verdant afterlife would truly seem like paradise to desert dwellers! And by the way, green is the color of Islam—an interesting and understandable choice for a religion born of the desert.)

Because of his iconoclastic teachings, Mohammed was driven from Mecca in 622 and fled to the city of Medina, where he was welcomed. The flight of Mohammed is called the *Hegira,* and 622 is the first year of the Muslim calendar. Mohammed gained many adherents during the years he spent in Medina, and eventually, these Muslims, led by Mohammed, conquered Mecca in 630 and brought it into the Islamic fold. In Mecca Mohammed removed the tribal idols from the *Kaaba* and dedicated it exclusively to Allah. He thus maintained the central importance of Mecca, and it remained—and remains—a city of pilgrimage. In the following two years most of the peoples of the Arabian Peninsula were converted to Islam.

When we consider Islam, we should note how perfectly tailored it is for mobile, desert-dwelling people, for no matter where they were, they could practice Islam. There are but five "pillars" or tenets:

1.  One may become a Muslim by reciting The Creed: "There is no God but Allah, and Mohammed is His Prophet."

2.  A Muslim should pray five times a day in the direction of Mecca.

3.  One should make a *hajj,* a pilgrimage to Mecca once in his lifetime. If unable to do so, he should make a donation to someone who can.

4.  A Muslim should give alms to the poor.

5.   A Muslim should fast during the daylight hours of the month of Ramadan.

Although Muslims did (and do) have houses of worship—*mosques*—with *imam*s who lead the faithful in prayer and deliver sermons, attendance is not mandatory under the Five Pillars of Faith.

Mohammed's followers memorized or wrote down his teachings, which were eventually collected into the Koran, or "recitation," about twenty years after his death. The Koran contains 114 verses, and is arranged from the longest verse to the shortest. Because the Koran is written in Arabic, it is incumbent on a true believer to learn this language in order to read the Koran in its original form.

# The Spread of Islam; Islamic Civilization (700–1100)

Once Arabia was converted to Islam, Muslims filled with the *jihad*, or holy-war spirit, swept out of the peninsula to conquer new territories in the name of Allah. Although relatively few in numbers, the zeal with which these Muslims fought, coupled with the speed and discipline of their forces, allowed them to subdue North Africa, Spain, Syria and Persia. The Arabs left intact the political structure of most of the conquered areas and dealt relatively leniently with those peoples that accepted Islam. Jews and Christians, deemed "People of the Book" (believers in God's word as revealed in the Bible), were theoretically given special treatment.

From 700–1100 Islamic civilization flourished. Muslim scholars drew on the learning of the empire's peoples and fused this knowledge with their own scholarship, creating a vibrant intellectual climate. In their intellectual zeal, they preserved many works from Ancient Greece, Persia and the Byzantine Empire. A Muslim mathematician developed algebra—the "bringing together of separate parts"—and other scholars' works led to a deeper understanding of geography, anatomy, and chemistry. Medical treatment was very sophisticated for this era. For example, Rhazes, a physician and prolific writer, drew on Greek, Indian, and Persian sources, as well as his own observations, to accurately describe various ailments. Some believe that Rhazes was the first doctor to use plaster casts to set broken limbs and to stitch wounds using animal gut. Other physicians performed cataract and cranial surgeries. In the realm of literature, the much-loved *Arabian Nights* took shape, as well as Omar Khayyan's great *Rubaiyat*. Finally, a distinctive form of architecture emerged during this period, synthesizing Byzantine domes and arches, Persian decorative motifs, and Islamic ideas. We need only think of the Taj Mahal in India or the Alhambra Palace in Spain to appreciate the enormous spread of the Islamic empire, and its profound impact on architecture and other forms of culture.

So how does Islam connect with our history of the West? Certainly Muslim Spain became a great center of learning, and Cordoba was the equivalent of Constantinople in the scope of its scholarship. Eventually some of this learning found its way over the Pyrenees into Western Europe. And, as stated at the chapter's beginning, the Islamic civilization preserved scholarship from Greece, Rome, and other cultures, and made significant achievements in a myriad of disciplines that would have a later impact on European civilization.

# 5

## The Middle Ages
## 500–1350

## The Early Middle Ages: Feudalism, Manorialism, the Church (500–1000)

The Middle Ages refers to the period between the fall of Rome and the Renaissance, a stretch of approximately 800 years. Although the term "Dark Ages" has gone out of vogue, it nonetheless remains an apt description for the first part of the Middle Ages. From roughly 500 to 1000, the order and safety provided by Rome was lost, as was much of the technology, trade, and scholarship. Urban life all but disappeared, and most people lived out their lives in squalid villages, never venturing far from home. During this period Germanic tribes, then Huns and Vikings pushed into large areas of Central and Western Europe, causing widespread devastation and misery. Rome's vast empire became the game board of nobles and chieftains who fought to carve out a secure area to call their own. Indeed, warfare was the foremost activity of the early Middle Ages.

During these turbulent times feudalism, the political and social system of the Middle Ages, developed to provide security and order in peoples' lives; manorialism, the economic system arising from life on manors, evolved to feed and clothe them; and the Church increased its power by filling many essential roles.

The feudal system evolved during the early Middle Ages. With the dissolution of the Roman Empire and the disappearance of a universal monetary system, land became the primary means of exchange, and was awarded as compensation for military service. Thus a powerful leader would grant a *fief*, a large tract of land, to each of his most important military supporters. These great landowners—often called dukes or counts—would then grant land to the lesser nobles who supported them. Over time a feudal hierarchy evolved, an intricate system of obligations and responsibilities between lords—those granting land—and vassals—those receiving land. (As you might imagine, it was possible to be both a lord and a vassal.) The king was theoretically at the apex of this hierarchy, and he was the vassal of God. Feudalism provided some stability and structure for the nobles, the upper 10 percent of society, during these perilous times; each noble knew where, in general, he stood in the (loosely) pyramid-shaped feudal structure and what his responsibilities entailed.

Feudal culture focused on combat, for the medieval knight and his horse were a fighting machine, at the ready to engage in battle. However, when not fighting tribal invaders, the knights were busy fighting each other. In fact, so frequent was warfare that the Church issued a proclamation in the eleventh century to restrict fighting to a few hours and days of the week. When not engaged in actual combat, knights often jousted against each other or engaged in large-scale tournaments, each eager to demonstrate his prowess, at risk to life and limb.

There were several distinct rites of passage to become a knight. From age seven to 14, a young boy of noble birth served as a page, usually in another lord's household. The lord expected him to so his bidding as page, and the lady of the manor instructed him in manners, Christian principles, and skills such as dancing and singing. From age 14 to 21 he served as a squire, assisting a knight and learning warrior skills. At age 21 he had the opportunity to become a knight if, among other requirements, he could mount his charger while wearing 100 pounds of armor! As the Middle Ages evolved, a chivalric code developed governing the behavior of the knight to other knights, as well as his behavior to women. He was supposed to be loyal, courageous, and honorable in combat, and polite and protective towards women, idealizing their beauty and grace.

And what of women's status in this feudal society? In general, women were considered inherently corrupt—one only had to consider the temptress Eve, mother of all women. Legally, women were under the charge of either their fathers or brothers or husbands, and thus had little independence. Moreover, noble women were frequently used as bargaining chips to forge an alliance with another family, to increase land holdings, and to garner power for their family of origin. Of course, in reality, women had some influence and were major contributors to medieval society: noblewomen ran their households and frequently supervised the manors when their husbands were absent; peasant women tended to their homes and usually worked side-by-side with their families in the fields. Additionally, the chivalric code, with its emphasis on female virtues, did help to elevate the status of noble women during the latter part of the Middle Ages.

While feudalism ensured some political and social order for the upper classes during the Middle Ages, manorialism provided for the economic needs of all, as well as some security for the peasants, the ninety percent of the population who lived on manors and worked the soil. Each manor had to be self-sufficient because trade had ceased, for the most part, and peasant smiths, tanners, millers, and coopers were essential to the manor's functioning.

A feudal lord governed his manor—some lords had several that they frequented throughout the year—and the peasants lived in the village near the manor house. In return for the lord's protection and for his dispensing justice during these dangerous times, the peasants tilled the land and paid him in kind. Generally they tended to the lord's fields three days a week and to their own fields for three days. On Sunday they attended church and ostensibly had a day of rest. In addition to working their lord's land, the peasants were often responsible for maintaining local roads and bridges at the lord's behest.

It is safe to say that life was miserable for the peasantry during this period. For example, they heated their small huts with a fire in the middle of their main (and often only) room. Smoke escaped through a hole in the center of the roof, but the hovels remained smoky, leading to constant eye irritation. Almost everyone had fleas and lice and suffered from malnutrition much of the time, especially during the winter months when fresh fruits and vegetables were scant. Peril in the form of wild beasts or vagabonds lurked in the forests beyond the manor, and these dangers, as well as lack of transportation, made it rare for a peasant to venture more than five miles from home during his lifetime.

In these difficult times, the Church emerged as the most important institution of the Middle Ages: it helped to provide stability in the lives of peasants and nobles alike, and offered the prospect of a brighter future in the next world. The Church controlled the path to salvation, and the desire to attain salvation—eternal life in Heaven—was the overwhelming concern for most people during this era. As you can imagine, the Church's control over the gateway to Heaven gave it enormous power. The mere threat of excommunication—denying a person participation in the sacraments—brought many a nobleman and peasant to heel. Additionally, the Church was the largest landowner in Europe, controlling one-quarter of the land. In a time when land represented power and wealth, the Church was, indeed, the most influential institution of the period.

In a very immediate way the Church, too, was an integral part of daily life. At the local level, each village had a priest and church that were central to all aspects of life. Church law helped regulate behavior, and the local priest was present and necessary for all of life's key passages: baptism, marriage, and death. The Church also provided for the social needs of villagers through its religious services, festivals, and pageants.

Beginning in the sixth century, a monastic movement developed within the Church for those seeking a life devoted to God. In the early 500s St. Benedict pledged himself to a life of "poverty, chastity and obedience" and these Benedictine laws, as they came to be called, provided the basis for monastic life. A monk lived with others in a monastery, headed by an abbot, and his life was spent in closely regulated hours of prayer, study, manual labor and rest. These monasteries contributed enormously to the life of the Middle Ages. They became centers of learning to ensure that the monks could read and write, thus keeping literacy alive during this "dark" era. Many monasteries preserved scholarship by directing the monks to copy ancient manuscripts; other monks recorded current events, providing us with wonderful and informative accounts of the past. Monasteries also provided refuge for the sick, the poor, and travelers.

At roughly the same time, convents developed as places where women could spend their lives away from the secular world, devoting themselves to God. In truth, a convent was frequently a haven for a woman who did not want to marry, who craved some freedom, or who wanted to pursue intellectual activities. Thus many talented, independent women elected to become nuns.

# The Art of the Period

Medieval art appears very different from the art of Classical times. In paintings, people no longer look realistic: they are generally flat rather than rounded, are outlined in black, and possess little individualization. Attempts at perspective in paintings and sculpture seem clumsy at best. However, the purpose of this art was different from earlier times: during the Middle Ages artists sought to depict the eternal Word of God and to illustrate it in a manner easily understood by the illiterate populace. For their aims, realism was neither important nor essential.

There were other differences between Classical and medieval art. As you might expect, during the Middle Ages religious themes and motifs prevailed over the secular subjects of the Classical era. Artists also ceased to sign their names to their works, reflecting the emphasis on community rather than the individual and highlighting the notion that one's accomplishments in this world are insignificant compared to his life in the next.

However, the decorative art of the period, ranging from embellished books like the Lindisfarne Gospels, to metal-worked items, are often amazing in their intricacy and imagination.

# Two "Lights" in the Dark: Charlemagne and Alfred the Great

## Charlemagne (742–814)

Charles the Great, or "Charlemagne," was one of the most outstanding individuals of his time—or any time, for that matter—and was truly a "light" in the Dark Ages. He came from an energetic and capable family that had ruled the area of France for several generations; his grandfather, Charles "the Hammer" Martel, had defeated Muslim invaders in 732, sending them back over the Pyrenees into Spain.

Charlemagne ruled from 768–814, and during this time he established an empire that included modern-day France, Austria, Belgium, the Netherlands, Germany and part of Italy. Not until Napoleon, one thousand years later, would so much of Europe be under the sway of a single individual! Records suggest that Charlemagne was very tall for his era—6'3"—with a broad build, ruddy complexion, and an intelligent and cheerful demeanor. He was an ardent Christian, dispensing charity with great zeal and attending church services twice a day. He was also absolutely ruthless in battle and once crucified 4,000 Saxons who refused to convert to Christianity. The pope crowned him Holy Roman Emperor on Christmas Day in 800, acknowledging his deep religious conviction ("Holy") and the extent of his domain ("Roman" as in Roman Empire).

Although Charlemagne was a bold military leader who led over 50 campaigns during his lifetime, he was also an impressive political administrator, astutely building on the work of his forebears. He divided his empire into 300 counties, with a count, duke, and bishop each responsible for running different aspects of the county. He sought to appoint wise and capable administrators and checked on their activities by sending out (and frequently rotating) royal inspectors, his "eyes and ears," as they were called. Moreover, he decreed that the managers of his royal farms send him detailed assessments of the royal property, down to the smallest item. He also promulgated laws that were a blend of Germanic tribal law and Christian principles.

In addition to his military and administrative prowess, Charlemagne had a deep love of learning, and his passion for such led to a period known as the Carolingian Renaissance. He ordered, for example, that each cathedral must establish a school to educate the clergy, some of whom were illiterate, and he encouraged monasteries to educate local boys of promise, no matter what their social class.

He also urged the monks to copy ancient manuscripts in order to preserve the scholarship of the past. He established a school at his capital in Aachen to educate his own children and those of the nobility. Additionally, he invited the leading scholars of the day to court, and he loved nothing better than a stimulating conversation or debate.

Although Charlemagne prized learning—he spoke Latin and a bit of Greek—he never learned to write. According to his friend and biographer Einhard, Charlemagne kept a tablet under his pillow to practice his writing, but having attempted to do so too late in life, he met with little success. The hand that wielded the sword was unable to develop the fine motor skills necessary to wield the pen. It is a moving vision, isn't it, that of Charlemagne, valiant military leader, efficient administrator, and vibrant intellect, diligently attempting to form his letters night after night, never mastering this one skill.

Charlemagne's heirs did not possess his military or administrative talents, and in 843 his grandsons divided his empire into thirds. The western part of his empire would eventually become France and the eastern part, called for generations the Holy Roman Empire, ultimately became Germany. Although his empire dissolved within 40 years of his death, Charlemagne's genius, coupled with his passion for learning, kept the flame of scholarship alive during the Dark Ages and helped preserve for posterity many great works from ancient times. His well-run empire also created a model on which future generations might draw.

## Alfred the Great (849–899)

We now move to England, where, in the generation after Charlemagne, an outstanding military leader, administrator and intellect arose: Alfred the Great, the only English king to have "great" affixed to his name.

By the ninth century the various Germanic tribes that had overrun England during the fifth and sixth centuries—Angles, Saxons and Jutes—had coalesced, to some degree, into a people who thought of themselves as English. Although they lived in separate kingdoms like Wessex, Sussex, and East Anglia, they called their island home "England"—land of the Angles. Over the years, these Anglo-Saxons developed several practices that would evolve into important English institutions. One of these was a rudimentary trial system with a noble or *thegn* acting as judge and 12 commoners, or *doomsmen*, serving as jury. Although the judgments or *dooms* were often harsh, this concept of trial-by-one's peers is key part of the Western legal system.

The Anglo-Saxon peoples faced their greatest challenge throughout the eighth and ninth centuries as Vikings from Denmark launched innumerable attacks on them, often defeating them and laying waste the countryside. It was during these turbulent times that Alfred, heir to the throne of Wessex, ascended to power at age 21.

Alfred demonstrated great talent from his earliest years. A story has it that his mother promised a reward to whomever of her five sons first learned to read. Alfred, the youngest, was the first to achieve this, and was given a book of Anglo-Saxon verse. He never lost this early drive for learning and his love of scholarship.

When Alfred inherited the throne of Wessex in 871, the Danes had conquered most of England and were threatening his borders. Alfred bought a truce from the Danes at great cost and used the time to develop a better army, to construct a strong navy and to build forts at strategic points. After four years the Danes attacked Wessex once again, and although Alfred lost several battles, he ultimately defeated the Danes and agreed that they could remain in a section of northeastern England called the Danelaw. (The Danes quieted down, farmed, married, and over the years became "English.")

With the defeat of the Danes, all the English recognized Alfred as their national hero and king, and he proved himself as talented in peace as he was in war. In administering his kingdom Alfred demonstrated a skill akin to that of Charlemagne. For example, he created a standardized law code and traveled throughout his kingdom to ensure that justice was served. He invited scholars from all of Europe to England to reinvigorate his culture and to promote education after the long years of war. He helped translate many books from Latin into the vernacular, Anglo-Saxon, and he wrote a history of England from Roman times to his own day, the *Anglo-Saxon Chronicle*. He had a copy of this book placed in each cathedral and monastery, and decreed that important events should be recorded as they happened. The *Chronicle* was maintained for 250 years following his death and provides us with an abundance of information about this period in history.

Alfred's descendents, the Anglo-Saxon kings, built on his achievements and continued to administer England efficiently. The kings divided England into units called shires and appointed earls to run each shire. Each shire also had a shire-reeve (later "sheriff") who brought miscreants before a local court, headed by the aforementioned *thegn*.

Approximately 100 years after Alfred's death, the Danes briefly controlled England again until the arrival of William of Normandy, known as William the Conqueror. William, too, was of Viking lineage—Normandy was the "land of the Northmen" in northwestern France. William defeated the English King Harold at the Battle of Hastings in 1066 then ruthlessly brought the rest of England under his sway. William is one of the strong men of history who, with his iron will and bloody sword, united England, established an efficient and powerful central government and ensured through the Salisbury Oath that all men were directly loyal to him. William's kinsmen continued to rule England and large sections of France for several generations after his death.

## The High Middle Ages (1000–1350)

Around 1000 A.D., a flowering of medieval civilization occurred for several reasons. Of major importance was the fact that warfare subsided: the barbarian invasions that had unsettled Europe for centuries ceased, and the Church, through the Crusades, channeled men's energies away from combat with each other to an enemy outside of Europe. With less fear of attack, trade revived, and with trade, existing towns increased in size, and others developed. Towns needed administrators, lawyers, merchants, physicians—a host of professions that involved education. Through necessity, a town's cathedral school, the traditional center of education, became more comprehensive in scope to train these professionals, and some cathedral schools slowly evolved into universities. Universities admitted ambitious students from all classes, thereby increasing the ranks of the educated. Additionally, the crusaders' contact with the sophisticated and vibrant Byzantine and Muslim empires brought an infusion of learning into Europe. Finally, some outstanding popes and new monastic movements reignited religious passion throughout Europe, which led to new kinds of ecclesiastical thought and to an innovative type of architecture. Indeed, this was a vibrant period in the Middle Ages, one that most of us do not appreciate when we think of medieval times.

## The New Scholarship in the Age of Faith

During this period scholarship in several areas is especially worthy of note. The Crusaders' contact with the Byzantine and Muslim civilizations reintroduced Europe to the works of the Ancient Greeks and Romans. The law code of Justinian, for example, provided a basis for intense legal discussions (and later legal codes), ancient authors inspired new literary efforts, but of utmost importance were Aristotle's works. Aristotle's emphasis on logic and reason led to heated debate regarding the role of philosophy, theology, and faith in one's spiritual life. A group of dynamic intellectuals, the Scholastics, considered the issue of faith and reason: does a person's reason lead him to faith—or does faith lead him to understanding? Furthermore, Aristotle's emphasis on logic and observation contributed to the development of early science. Robert Grosseteste (1168–1253) and his famous pupil Roger Bacon (1214–1292) emphasized the importance of observation and experimentation; indeed, Bacon is often credited with laying the foundation of the modern scientific method.

This period, however, is also called "The Age of Faith." The Crusades, which began in 1096 and spanned 200 years, clearly illustrate the power of the Church during this era. When Pope Urban II issued the Call of Clermont in 1095, he enjoined the Christians of Europe to win back the Holy Land, which had fallen to the Muslim Turks. Over 100,000 people—kings, nobles, and common folk—responded to the pope's call to action in this, the First Crusade. Although religious zeal motivated many crusaders, opportunities for adventure or to acquire wealth were also strong incentives. On their way to the Holy Land, however, the crusaders pillaged and killed, and the Jews of Europe, especially, experienced their ruthlessness. This pattern of wreaking devastation would continue throughout the many Crusades—all in the name of God.

The Third Crusade, led in part by Richard the Lionhearted of England (ruled 1189–1199), remains one of the most famous crusades, primarily because of Richard's participation. Richard, a son of Henry II and a glamorous warrior-king, was arguably the best general of his time. He fought his way to the Holy Land and captured the Muslim stronghold of Acre, but ultimately failed to take Jerusalem. He and his formidable Muslim foe, Saladin, exchanged messages and presents and treated each other with respect. The charismatic Richard and his exploits gave rise to many legends among Christians as well as Muslims.

Moreover, two new vibrant monastic orders evolved during this time, the Franciscans and the Dominicans. Both orders represented a recommitment to the religious vows of poverty, chastity, and obedience. Saint Francis of Assisi (1181?–1226), a wealthy and by all accounts rather raucous youth, established the Franciscan order in the early thirteenth century. After a period of illness, he pledged to divest himself of his possessions and to help the poor. The example of his simple life, coupled with the sweetness of his nature, helped to make the Franciscan order one of the most popular.

## Heavenly Architecture: the Gothic Cathedral

It is, perhaps, the glorious Gothic cathedrals erected during this time that best symbolize the dynamism of the age, reifying both the secular and religious climate. A cathedral needed a flourishing town with its considerable wealth to support its construction. Affluent merchants, local guilds and average townspeople, as well as the Church itself, contributed to the building. For many donors, their contributions were acts of deep faith, for a cathedral often took one hundred years to construct and few people alive at its beginning would live to see its completion. Cathedrals were built with the simplest of tools, but designed by men who understood principles of engineering. Over the years cathedrals became increasingly taller; illuminated by large, beautiful stained glass windows, they were supported on the exterior by graceful flying buttresses. As a worshipper entered, he could not help but be awed by the building's magnificence. Even today we marvel at these architectural wonders constructed 1,000 years ago, enduring testaments to engineering genius—and to the faith of the age.

## Political Change in England (1066–1215)

Politically, noteworthy changes occurred during the High Middle Ages, particularly in England. Following the Norman invasion of 1066, William the Conqueror and his successors forged a strong central government and laid the foundation for many contemporary English institutions. William's two advisory councils, for example, the Great Council and the King's Council, eventually evolved into the two houses of the English Parliament. Additionally, during this period royal officials began to count taxes on checkered boards—thus the emergence of Britain's financial bureau, the office of the Exchequer. William's energetic grandson Henry II was especially interested in extending the system of royal justice and employed itinerant judges, who traveled the realm, to render justice. Because these judges began to rely on a "common law" when reaching a decision, people started to look to these royal courts to settle a case, rather than to the Church or baronial courts. As you might imagine, Henry's desire to use these courts to try wayward clergy eventually brought him into conflict with the Church, headed by his close friend Thomas Becket. Becket was assassinated—it is unclear to what extent Henry was responsible for his death—but the eventual result of this conflict was the growth of the royal courts and common law and a diminution in Church courts. Henry also strengthened central power in other ways, creating a paid, capable bureaucracy that would function smoothly, even in his absence. And he was away frequently, defending his family's lands in France: Normandy, inherited from William, and vast territory in central and southern France gained through his marriage to Eleanor of Aquitaine.

It was under Henry II's youngest son, King John (ruled 1199–1216), that one of the most significant events in English history occurred: the creation of the *Magna Carta* in 1215. John was an unpopular king: he had lost a nasty power struggle with the pope and had also lost much of Normandy to the French king. To compound matters, he had levied illegal taxes on his barons and other free subjects to subsidize his wars with France. Enraged, the barons drew up a "great charter" threatening war on John if he refused its terms. Although the barons sought to preserve their feudal privileges in the *Magna Carta*, they also included some very modern-sounding demands that extended beyond themselves to all free English men. For example: no tax could be levied without the approval of the Great Council; an arrested free man had the right to a speedy trial, and the trial must be by his peers; no free man's punishment should exceed his crime; no one could be tried more than once for the same offense; and the monarch must respect a town's charter, which guaranteed it certain liberties—all this in 1215! With the *Magna Carta*, we begin to see the emergence of the idea that a person possesses certain rights—an idea central to the West, and one that would gather momentum in England and the rest of Europe over the centuries.

Beyond the specifics of this seminal document, two revolutionary principles evolved: that the king was *not* above the law—a startling concept for the time—and that he must consult with Parliament (here called the Great Council) before levying taxes.

## A Grim End: The Black Death

Finally, we cannot conclude this chapter without noting one of the most catastrophic events that ever struck Europe: the bubonic plague, more often called the Black Death, of 1348–1351. Historians estimate that one-third to one-half the population of Europe perished as a result of the plague (called the Black Death because its victims developed spots of blood under their skin, which often turned black). The plague had enormous effects on Europe: a shortage of workers led to economic decline, the death of many town officials led to a breakdown in government, and desperation filled the lives of all. It would take fully one hundred years for Europe to recover from its ravages.

# Overview

# The Early Modern Era
# 1350–1550

## What Do We Mean by "Early Modern"?

Three great movements—the Renaissance, the Age of Exploration and the Reformation—served to advance Europe into the early modern age. What are some of the characteristics that we think of as "early modern" that developed during this period? Foremost is the emphasis placed on the dignity and significance of the individual, and the value placed on his accomplishments in his earthly life. This is very different from the medieval view that a person was but a tiny cog in the vast universe whose focus should be on attainting salvation. Additionally, secular interests, especially curiosity about the physical world, began to compete with the focus on religion. People also started to challenge authority and tradition, and the Church, in particular, came under attack. And, to some degree, a sense of national identity began to emerge among some of the European peoples. They began to think of themselves as Spanish, English, or French, rather than Christians united by the universal Church.

# 6

# *The Renaissance 1350–1550*

## The Early Italian Renaissance (1350–1450)

The Renaissance began in Italy during the 1300s. After the long stretch of the Middle Ages, the people of the Renaissance came to believe that they were the heirs to the intellectual and artistic achievements of Ancient Greece and Rome—thus the notion of renaissance, or rebirth. They embraced the idea of humanism, i.e., a renewed belief in the worth and dignity of the individual and on the importance of his life in this world, rather than in the next. As William Shakespeare so aptly expressed:

> "What a piece of work is man, how noble in reason,
>
> How infinite in faculties,
>
> In form and moving, how express and admirable,
>
> In action, how like an angel,
>
> In apprehension, how like a god."[1]

The Italian Petrarch (1304–1374) is often called the "founder of humanism." Although many of his writings had a religious, medieval cast to them, he nonetheless was deeply engaged in the matters of this world, and more than any other individual of his time, he promoted the study of the ancient authors. Additionally, during this time scholars began to emphasize the importance of studying secular subjects like poetry, history, and rhetoric—subjects that they called the humanities.

---

1.  *Hamlet*, II, ii, 303–312.

The Renaissance began in Italy for a host of reasons. Italy's geographic position, a peninsula projecting into the Mediterranean, put it at the crossroads of traffic, ideal for the exchange of goods and of ideas. Additionally, feudalism had never taken deep hold in Italy; rather, this area had evolved into a patchwork of city-states, in which powerful families, most often wealthy merchants, governed a city and its environs. The urban tradition had thus survived more fully in Italy, in places like Florence, Venice, Siena and Milan. Wealthy patrons of the arts, like the Medici of Florence, vied to entice the best artists and architects to come and work in their cities, thus fueling the accomplishments of the era. Moreover, the Italian peoples bore daily witness to the architectural and artistic achievements of Ancient Rome—statuary, aqueducts, coliseums—that served as reminders of their past greatness and as inspiration for future achievement. Finally, many scholars fled to Italy when Constantinople came under siege from the Turks in the 1450s, adding to the intellectual vibrancy of this time.

The Italian Renaissance is generally divided into two periods, the Early Italian Renaissance, roughly 1350–1450, and the High Italian Renaissance, 1450–1550. Although many significant writers emerged during this time period, the Renaissance spirit found its greatest expression in art. During the Early Renaissance artists moved away from the artistic conventions and limitations of the Middle Ages. During the Middle Ages, human subjects were generally drawn in a flat, non-individualized manner; flora and fauna were unrealistic and efforts to render perspective were clumsy at best. Religion, as you might suspect, provided the greatest inspiration for art during this time. Around 1350, an interest in the natural world took hold when artists strove to create more realistic people and settings. Artists such as Leonardo da Vinci and Michelangelo defied Church teachings by studying dissected human bodies in order to paint and sculpt the human form more accurately. The artist and architect Brunelleschi determined the mathematical principles governing perspective, allowing artists to render distant objects more realistically. And although religious themes continued to be significant throughout the Renaissance, artists also drew on ancient mythology, as well as on people and events from everyday life, as inspiration for their works. Artists began to sign their works, indicating a movement away from the communal mentality of the Middle Ages toward a celebration of the individual and his talents.

Giotto (1266–1337) is considered the first painter to break with some of the artistic conventions of the Middle Ages. The figures in his paintings are more individualized and expressive than medieval works, and he employs a rudimentary sense of perspective through his technique of foreshortening. (Foreshortening means that an object in the distance appears smaller than an object in the foreground.) Giotto, by the way, also designed the bell tower in Florence, the famous *campanile*. His expertise in painting and in architecture illustrates the talent in several areas that Renaissance individuals often possessed.

Following Giotto were such painters as Masaccio (1401–1428), who is often heralded as the most proficient painter of the Early Renaissance; he effectively employed the technique of *chiaroscuro*—the use of light and shadow, rather than dark lines—to mold his figures. His people thus look rounded and natural in contrast to medieval works. Many of his paintings, such as Adam and Eve in *Expulsion From Paradise,* also depict profound human emotion. Another key painter from this period, Botticelli (1444–1510), frequently drew on ancient myth, rather than religious motifs, to paint his elongated, lovely nudes. *Venus Rising from the Sea* and *Primavera* are two of his best-known works. Donatello (1386–1466) was one of the most masterful Early Renaissance sculptors. His small bronze statue *David* was the first freestanding nude since Classical times. His other works, such as *Mary Magdalene*, portray great depth of emotion. Finally, we should also note the sculptor and architect Filippo Brunelleschi (1377–1446), the man credited with first understanding the laws of perspective, whose dome crowning the cathedral in Florence is a triumph of architectural and engineering daring.

## The High Renaissance in Italy (1450–1550)

Artists of the High Renaissance demonstrated even greater mastery in their quest to depict their subjects in a realistic manner. During this period artists gave more psychological dimension to their subjects, glorified the nude body, fully mastered the technique of perspective and embraced the idea of artist as genius.

Leonardo da Vinci (1452–1519), one of the foremost artists, was most certainly a genius. His great works *Mona Lisa* and *The Last Supper* continue to astonish people with their technical mastery and psychological depth. Moreover, his observations about the natural world, as well as his inventions, are testaments to his curiosity and intellect. Leonardo was among the first to propose that sound might travel through the air in waves, just as waves travel through water. He also believed that our vision was linked to the brain, not to rays that objects emitted, as was the customary view. He studied fossils and developed ideas that presaged the theory of evolution. He also made detailed illustrations for a flying machine, a rudimentary tank, and a sort of submarine. He committed many of his ideas to notebooks, in which he wrote backwards, right to left. (We are not certain why he did this.) His notebooks, however, were disorganized and went unpublished;

it was left for future generations to decipher his writings and to discover the depth of his intellect.

Michelangelo Buonarroti (1475–1564), another genius of the High Renaissance, was a sculptor, painter, architect and poet, whose fervent Christianity imbues all his work. His most famous pieces include the sculptures *The Pieta* and *David* and the ceiling painting of the Sistine Chapel. It took Michelangelo four years, lying on scaffolding 100 feet above the ground, to complete this project. His "Creation," in which God brings the spark of life to Adam, is one of the most celebrated of the ceiling's paintings. Michelangelo also designed the world's largest dome, that beautiful structure that adorns St. Peter's cathedral in Rome. To many of his contemporaries, this dome was the most important and impressive architectural feat of all time, and it remains so for many visitors to St. Peter's today.

Raffaello Santi, commonly called Raphael (1483–1520), is often accorded the most accomplished painter of the High Renaissance, and his renowned *School of Athens* epitomizes the hallmarks of the period: a mastery of perspective, the use of a secular subject and the rendering of highly individualized people. In fact, Raphael incorporated well-known people of his time into this piece, such as Leonardo, Michelangelo—and even himself; perhaps he is suggesting that artists are the true stars of his era. Raphael is also known for his beautiful paintings of the Madonna and Child. So admired was his work and of such sweet temperament was he, that when he died there was universal lamentation, and he was given the great honor of burial in the Pantheon in Rome.

Last to arrive on the scene was Titian (1487–1576), who used thick layers of paint and rich colors to create highly realistic works. Titian became the most popular portrait painter of his day, and in pieces such as *Man with the Glove* and *Paul III and His Grandsons*, we see not only remarkable mastery of oil painting, but also a deep understanding of his subjects' characters. So distinct is his color palette that "Titian red" refers to the shade that he used so frequently in his works.

During this time of artistic innovation, several important writers emerged in Renaissance Italy. Besides Petrarch, the aforementioned founder of humanism, we should also note Baldassarre Castiglione (1478–1529), whose *Book of the Courtier* described the ideal Renaissance man. The many qualities that he enumerated are those that, even today, constitute a well-rounded individual.

In the realm of literature, Giovanni Boccaccio (1313–1375) wrote his masterwork *The Decameron*. In 1348 Boccaccio witnessed the horrors of the Black Death in his native city of Florence, and shortly thereafter he wrote *The*

*Decameron.* In his book, 10 young men and women who have fled Florence during the plague recount 100 bawdy tales from their place of refuge in the country.

Perhaps the most significant political writer of this era was Niccolo Machiavelli (1469–1527). Indeed, we still use the term "Machiavellian" today to describe a person who will attempt to achieve a goal at any cost. In his book *The Prince*, Machiavelli identified the qualities necessary for a strong leader who, he hoped, might unite the Italian states against foreign invaders. In his view, a leader should be as powerful as a lion and as cunning as a fox. He contended that "it is better to be feared than be loved; for, in general, men are ungrateful, inconstant, hypocritical … and covetous of gain."[2] He believed that such practices as bribery and lying were necessary means to achieve the sort of power a strong prince should possess.

## The Northern Renaissance (1450–1600)

It took almost 100 years for the Renaissance to cross the Alps from Italy into the North. When it took hold, the Northern Renaissance differed from the Italian Renaissance in two major ways: in Northern Europe the nobles were generally patrons of the arts, in contrast to wealthy merchants, and religion continued to play a greater role there than it had in Italy.

Just as the Italian Renaissance had Petrarch to articulate the new humanist views, so the Northern Renaissance had the priest Erasmus of Rotterdam (1466–1536), sometimes called the "prince of humanists." Erasmus advocated a "Christian humanism" which called for a Christianity driven not by strict dogma but rather by ethics. He was critical of many aspects of the Church and of human behavior, and he often satirized both. One of his major achievements was translating the New Testament into Greek and Latin, the first such translation in 1,000 years.

Art, too, was central to the Northern Renaissance and foremost among the artists was the German Albrecht Durer (1471–1528), who twice traveled to Italy to study new artistic techniques. Durer made brilliant works in copper engravings, woodcuttings and paintings that represent a fusion of the Italian Renaissance, traditional German art, and religion. He brought realism and power to all his works, and his allegorical *The Knight, Death and the Devil* and *The Four Horsemen of the Apocalypse* are two of his most famous. Another German painter, Hans Holbein the Younger (1497–1543), was noted for his portraiture; fleeing to

---

2.    Howe and Howe, *Ancient and Medieval Worlds*, 574.

the English court during the Reformation, he became the favorite painter of Henry VIII. And in Flanders (the northern part of Belgium), the Breughels, both father and son, painted landscapes, long a Flemish tradition, as well as the lives of everyday folk.

The Northern Renaissance was also rich in literature. During this time Sir Thomas More (1478–1535), an English lawyer and humanist, wrote his masterpiece *Utopia*, which literally means "nowhere." In this work More discussed the ideal state, one in which private property has been abolished, and greed and pride, products of economic inequality, have disappeared. In his vision, material goods would be communally owned, and education would be coupled with reason. The resulting "utopia" would be a place of perfection. Because he believed in the inherent goodness of people and the possibility of creating such an ideal state, he is often contrasted to Machiavelli with his negative view of human nature.

It was during this time that the French writer and humanist Francois Rabelais (1494–1553) wrote brilliant satires; we still read and enjoy his *Gargantua and Pantagruel*, the story of two giants with huge appetites. Rabelais also contributed many new words to the French language. The Spaniard Miguel de Cervantes (1547–1616) wrote *Don Quixote*, the ageless tale of an idealistic knight and his steadfast squire, Sancho Panza, who set out to perform chivalrous deeds in an inhospitable world. The word "quixotic," derived from his tale, denotes someone who is capricious or impractical in the pursuit of ideals. And finally, the greatest of them all, William Shakespeare (1564–1616) wrote his many brilliant plays and poems in Elizabethan England.

Shakespeare's works demonstrate keen insight into human nature, a vast range of knowledge and a mastery of language. In fact, Shakespeare added many words to the English language, just as Rabelais did in French, and experts attribute such words such as "bump," "lonely," and "assassination" to him. We divide Shakespeare's plays—around 37 of them—into comedies, tragedies and histories. *Much Ado About Nothing*, *A Mid-Summer's Night Dream* and *The Taming of the Shrew* are some of his famous comedies; *Hamlet, Macbeth, Othello, Romeo and Juliet* and *King Lear*—those staples of high-school English class—are among his best tragedies. His sonnets, some addressed to a young nobleman and others to a "dark lady," often deal with themes of love, the quick passage of time and the loss of beauty and vitality.

Finally, we should note one of the most important inventions of this period that served to disseminate Renaissance ideas and to promote literacy: Johann Gutenberg's (1400–1468) printing press. By creating a press with movable type in the 1450s, Gutenberg made possible a more expedient way to print papers and books, thereby lowering their costs and allowing more readership. We should also note that the first book he published was the Bible; there are 48 partial and complete extant Gutenberg Bibles.

With these new humanistic ideals, we might suspect that traditional attitudes changed towards women, but, for the most part, they did not. Although there were a few celebrated women—Isabella d'Este (1474–1539), a great patron of the arts, and Sofonishba Anguissola (1531–1626), a fine artist—the cloister still represented a good choice for an independent, intelligent woman.

# 7

# *The Age of Discovery and Conquest 1350–1700*

## Europeans Explore the Globe

Beginning in the early 1400s Portugal and Spain began to subsidize voyages of exploration. Some historians have succinctly described the reasons behind these expeditions as "gold, God and glory." Indeed, the Iberian countries, and later other countries, were motivated to explore the globe by the desire for trade and wealth. They wanted, in particular, easier, cheaper, and more direct access to spices, perfumes, and silks from Asia, because Muslims and Italians controlled the trade routes. Additionally, the desire to spread Christianity motivated many of these voyages. In 1492 Ferdinand and Isabella, Spain's rulers, had completed the *Reconquista*, the reconquest of Spain from non-Christians, expelling both Muslims and Jews. They now desired to spread the "true" religion to other parts of the globe, as did some of the leaders of countries that would later follow suit. Furthermore, prestige accrued with each new discovery and with each addition of land to empire, and this desire for glory motivated Portugal, Spain, and later Britain, France, and the Netherlands. We should also note that curiosity about uncharted territories, in part driven by the Renaissance spirit, played into the impulse for exploration.

In addition to these underlying reasons, new technology—sturdier ships, an improved rudder, triangular sails—made these voyages possible. Also fueling the movement were men like Columbus, enterprising individuals who could shop around in Europe, seeking a patron to subsidize their dreams. Thus Columbus, for example, approached the kings of Portugal, France, and England before gaining the patronage of Isabella of Spain for his grand undertaking.

The Portuguese took the lead in the Age of Exploration with the strong support of Prince Henry the Navigator (1396–1460). Prince Henry established a navigation school in Portugal that attracted European cartographers, shipbuilders, instrument makers, and others dedicated to improving ships' travel. Additionally, he subsidized over 50 expeditions down the west coast of Africa. As the Portuguese sailed along the coast, they established many trading posts, and brought back precious items like ivory, gold, and, eventually, slaves. Over time, these bold sailors continued to push further along the uncharted coast, and it was the Portuguese Bartholomew Dias who first rounded the Cape of Good Hope in 1487. Another Portuguese captain, Vasco da Gama, reached India in 1498. His successful excursion opened India to the Portuguese and later to other Europeans.

However, it was the intrepid Christopher Columbus (1451–1506) who dared to venture into the unknown, away from the safety of coastlines—who headed west, hoping to reach the East. What an act of courage to set off with three small ships and motley crew into what was commonly called "the Sea of Darkness." After two months under sail, Columbus reached land, probably one of the islands in the Bahamas. He declared that he had reached the East and called the inhabitants of the island "Indians," after India. The Old World had met the New.

Following Columbus, the voyages of discovery accelerated: John and Sebastian Cabot, sailing for England, explored the North American coast from 1497–1498 and established the basis for England's claim to this area. Ferdinand Magellan's Spanish expedition circumnavigated the globe from 1519–1522 and laid claim to the Philippines for Spain. The French explored and mapped some of eastern Canada, as well as the area around the Great Lakes and the Mississippi River, establishing French rights to these lands.

## Conquest and Colonization

Discovery and claiming often resulted in conquest and colonization. The Portuguese claimed and settled Brazil, and also extended their trading empire throughout the Indian Ocean, capturing and conquering towns from India to the Spice Islands (Indonesia). They returned to Europe with spices and other goods, selling their wares for one-fifth the cost charged by the Italians and Arab Muslims. Their good fortune eventually inspired Britain and the Netherlands, in particular, to contest Portuguese dominance. Britain ultimately gained control of India, and the Dutch ousted and replaced the Portuguese in Indonesia and South Africa. Both the British and the Dutch colonized these areas; the many Indian restaurants in England and Indonesian restaurants in the Netherlands attest to the continued relationship between these areas.

In the New World, the Spanish *conquistadors,* in their zeal to find rumored cities of gold, battled many native Indian peoples, leaving a swath of devastation. In 1521 Hernando Cortez laid waste to the Aztecs of Mexico, and in 1532 Francisco Pizarro conquered the Incas of Peru. Spain eventually claimed California, Mexico, and the rest of Central America, as well as Cuba and much of South America. The Spanish developed huge estates in their New World territories, worked by African and Indian slaves; they also established universities, missions, and churches. It is worth noting that in these Spanish lands, as well as in Portuguese Brazil, intermarriage among the different groups was accepted more readily than it would be in North America; *mestizos,* or mixed-race peoples, are much more common today in South America than in North America.

## Effects of the Age of Discovery

The results of this movement were many and profound. For one, the Age of Discovery initiated Europe's domination of the globe, a domination that would last into the 20$^{th}$ century. It increased the wealth of many nations, especially the Netherlands and Britain, and inaugurated a commercial revolution, as joint stock companies emerged to take advantage of the increased trade and rising affluence. Oddly enough, for a variety of reasons, Spain and Portugal ended up losing money by the end of the 1600s, and went into an extended period of economic decline.

Furthermore, new products were introduced from the New World into Europe: tomatoes, potatoes, chocolate, and tobacco, to name but a few of the most significant. It is interesting to note that crops we associate with some European countries—the tomato with Italy and the potato with Ireland, for example—were actually native to the New World. Traveling the other way, crops like wheat, and animals such as the horse, cow, and pig, went from Europe to the Americas.

The contact with new peoples and their cultures greatly expanded the horizons of Europeans. This contact would eventually foster new, more relativistic attitudes that would find full flower during the period of the Enlightenment.

There were also many tragic consequences to this period. Disease found its way across the Atlantic from Europe, and millions of the American peoples died from such scourges as small pox, influenza and diphtheria. Additionally, millions of Africans died in human trafficking, when slaves became one of the most lucrative cargoes. The Portuguese introduced African slaves into Europe, but after 1500 the largest markets emerged in the New World. The Spanish and Portuguese brought slaves into their territories in the Indies and South America, while the British, and to some extent the Dutch, transported African slaves to their holdings in the Caribbean and North America. Between 9.5 and 12 million men, women, and children survived the terrible Middle Passage across the ocean, and countless others perished during the ordeal. Slavery fractured families and deprived Africa of many of its strongest individuals; its deleterious effects on Africa cannot be overstated.

# 8

# *The Reformation 1517 and Beyond*

## Background to the Reformation

The institution that had bound Europeans together for 1,000 years, the Church, had come under attack throughout its history. Its power and wealth, as well as the corruption of some of its clergy, made it a clear, if formidable, target for reformers. Although the Church had responded to some of these calls for change, many of the foremost challengers—men like Jan Hus (1369–1415)—were charged with heresy and burned at the stake. Others were forced to recant their beliefs or face excommunication and house arrest.

However, by the early 1500s, the climate in Europe was more supportive of challenges to the Church. The secularism and individualism fostered by the Renaissance, the emergence of kings and princes who viewed the Church as a competitor, and a growing sense of nationalism among Europeans who gave their loyalties to a prince or king rather than a pope, contributed to the success of the movement known as the Reformation. The new invention of the printing press also helped to disseminate Reformation ideas.

The Reformation began in the Holy Roman Empire, the approximate region of Germany today. The Holy Roman Empire, headed by an emperor, consisted of many semi-autonomous states led by princes, many of whom sought more independence from both the pope and the emperor. Also, by 1500 the people of this area were beginning to think of themselves as Germans and had waning allegiance to a pope and Church centered in distant Italy.

# Martin Luther and Protestantism

The German priest and lawyer, Martin Luther (1483–1546), initiated the Reformation by attacking certain practices of the Church (which we should now think of as the Roman Catholic Church). Luther became outraged over the sale of indulgences in Germany, papers that were marketed with the spurious claim that they ensured forgiveness of sins and hence an easier passage to Heaven. Luther also felt that the sale of indulgences was a ploy to raise revenue from poor German folk to subsidize the construction of the dome for St. Peter's in Rome, a cathedral most of them would never see. He posted his points of contention, the 95 Theses, on the door of the Wittenberg Cathedral in 1517, and his protest inaugurated the reform movement.

Over the next few years Luther disseminated his ideas through a plethora of publications. He was Christian, yes, but he called for practices that diverged from those of the Catholic Church. Luther dispensed with the necessity of priests, for in reality, he argued, each individual was his own priest and could communicate directly with God. Luther further argued that the Bible was the only source of religious truth, and that a person could apprehend that truth himself. He contended that salvation came through faith alone, not through faith and good works as the Catholic Church maintained. He also alleged that communion and baptism were the only two sacraments, challenging the Church's belief in seven sacraments. Finally, he asserted that priests could marry, which he himself did in 1525. Because Luther protested against many key Catholic beliefs, this new branch of Christianity was called Protestantism.

Luther was, of course, excommunicated from the Catholic Church and in 1521 was declared an "outlaw of the realm." Following this judgment a sympathetic German prince hid Luther for a year, and during this period Luther translated the New Testament into German, allowing access to it for the many Germans who did not speak Latin or Greek. Luther is often called the father of the German language because of this translation and others.

# The Reformation Spreads

Eventually, some of the German princes and much of the population supported Luther's idea. In 1524 many German peasants, inspired by Luther's emphasis on the equality of all believers, broadened this idea to encompass social equality. They rebelled against the local landowners, looting and burning estates and sometimes murdering the occupants. Authorities dealt ruthlessly with the bloody

Peasant Revolt of 1524–1525, and Luther backed the authorities; ironically, he was a religious revolutionary but a social conservative. His support of the status quo resulted in some loss of peasant support for Lutheranism, as his type of Protestantism was called. Many peasants returned to the Catholic Church or joined other emerging Protestant sects.

Luther's ideas also incited religious wars that plagued the Holy Roman Empire for several decades; Protestant princes fought against Catholic princes over which form of Christianity should prevail. Finally, in 1555, the Peace of Augsburg decreed that each German prince had the right to choose which form of Christianity his principality would follow, Catholicism or Lutheranism. Note that individuals within each state had no say in the decision—they were expected to follow the decision made by their head of state. Nor were any of the newer Protestant sects recognized, only Lutheranism.

Inspired by Luther's success, other individuals took up the Reformation's call. John Calvin, a Swiss-born lawyer and priest, embraced most of Luther's ideas, but added a major one of his own: Calvin espoused the idea of "the elect," that is, the belief that God has predetermined a select few to be saved. He contended that sometimes it is possible identify these lucky few, for they have been blessed with economic prosperity. This idea, that wealth was a positive sign, helped to develop the idea of the "Protestant work ethic," since hard work often brought prosperity. Calvinism influenced many Europeans; one of Calvin's followers, John Knox, carried his beliefs into Scotland and established the Presbyterian Church there. Over time, many other Protestant sects emerged; in addition to Lutherans, Calvinists, and Presbyterians, there were Baptists, Congregationalists, Episcopalians and Methodists.

As Protestantism spread across Europe, it found more adherents in northern Europe than in the south, where Catholicism was deeply entrenched. The Scandinavian countries, the Netherlands, sections of Belgium, and eventually England, too, entered into the Protestant fold. In France, a minority of the citizenry embraced Protestantism. These Huguenots, as they were called, were harassed and murdered, and ultimately many fled France for more hospitable countries.

## Henry VIII and the English Reformation

The Tudor king Henry VIII (1491–1547) brought the Reformation to England in 1534.

He was desperate for a male heir, and his first wife, Catherine of Aragon, had presented him with only one child, Mary, after 16 years of marriage. Henry wanted to divorce Catherine in order to marry the lovely, vivacious, and young Anne Boleyn. When the Pope denied Henry's request for a divorce, Henry broke with Catholicism, declared himself head of the Church of England, divorced Catherine and married Anne. His rupture with the Catholic Church was thus for political, not religious, purposes.

So how did the people of England respond to Henry's actions? Some of them clung fervently to Catholicism, but the majority followed Henry's lead: they were loyal to their king, and his Anglican Church, the Church of England, appealed to their growing sense of nationalism. Additionally, they were aware of the corruption in the Catholic Church, a church headed by a distant pope. Also, the Anglican church service remained very similar to the Catholic service, so the transition to Protestantism was relatively smooth. Furthermore, Henry mollified the nobles and gentry by eventually allowing them to purchase large parcels of Church land, thereby increasing their estates.

## The Catholic Church Responds

The Catholic Church reacted to the Protestant threat with vigor and reexamined its beliefs and practices. As a result of the Council of Trent, a major convocation held from 1545–1563, it reaffirmed its core beliefs and attempted to deal with areas of corruption. Additionally, Ignatius Loyola founded a new and fervent religious order, the Jesuits, during this period; the Jesuits called themselves "soldiers of Christ," ready to serve the Pope and Catholicism.

In essence, however, the monolithic, universal Church was broken and would never again wield such power over the peoples of the West.

# 9

# *Major States in the Seventeenth Century*

In the three previous chapters we have looked at major movements that provided a transition from the Middle Ages to a more modern Europe. In this chapter we will pause to look at the political situation in five European states and in America during the 1600s, and we will also make some generalizations about the life of the people during this era.

Europe in the seventeenth century was fraught with wars and rebellions, with economic depression and famine, and with social violence that found its greatest expression in the witch hunt craze. Against this tumultuous backdrop, however, significant political developments occurred. During this period France and England became powerful and wealthy nations; both were central players in European politics and continued to wield power on the world stage into the twentieth century. The Austrian Empire, forged by the Habsburgs in the late 1600s, played a significant role in European politics for several hundred years. The Holy Roman Empire and Russia, although not especially significant at this point in history, would emerge as major forces in the late nineteenth and twentieth centuries and their origins, therefore, are of interest.

What of other European countries? Spain and Portugal entered a prolonged period of decline during the 1600s that extended into the twentieth century. The Italian peninsula was divided into areas controlled by some European powers, the Church, and a few Italian families, rendering it politically weak. The Netherlands emerged as a flourishing nation during this period, but its diminutive size and some political issues rendered it a minor player on the European stage.

Across the Atlantic in America, the English colonies attracted increasing numbers of English, Scotch-Irish, Germans, and other Europeans during the 1600s. The intrepid and ambitious folk who braved the Atlantic crossing, coupled with

America's abundant natural resources, created a thriving new world filled with promise.

# The Thirty Years' War (1618–1648)

Before discussing the significant states of the 1600s, we must briefly describe one of the most devastating events to engulf Europe, the Thirty Years' War of 1618–1648. The war began in the Holy Roman Empire over religious and political issues: Protestant princes and their supporters battled the Catholic Emperor Ferdinand II, a member of the powerful Habsburg family, and his Catholic allies. This civil war eventually brought in other European powers. Some nations, like Sweden, entered the fray primarily because of strong Protestant conviction, while others, like Spain, joined the conflict to fight on behalf of Catholicism (and in Spain's case, to support its German Habsburg relatives). France, although a Catholic country, felt threatened by strong Habsburg states on either side, and eventually fought against both. Although the conflict drew in many European countries, most of the combat took place in the German states, which were ravaged over the 30-year period. Armies destroyed villages and towns, burned fields, and slaughtered livestock; indeed, historians estimate that one-third of the German population perished during this time.

The war ended with the Peace of Westphalia in 1648, a treaty that was the product of the first general European peace conference. It was during this conference that the concept emerged of establishing international order through diplomatic solutions.

# Major European States

# France

During the 1600s France was the most affluent European nation, led by a strong king who legitimized his rule with the divine-right theory: a monarch was considered "God's lieutenant on Earth." Louis XIV, who ruled France from 1643–1715, declared "I am the state," and his appellation "the sun king" was apt, for all of society revolved around him. With abundant skill he kept potential threats to his power—the Church and army, for example—in check. Additionally, he kept the nobles under close watch at the fabulous palace of Versailles, and he rewarded capable middle-class men, the bourgeoisie, with important government positions in an effort to garner their support. Under Louis, the French court was the most dazzling in Europe, and other monarchs sought to emulate the French style.

However, there were deep-seated issues within French society and among the most significant was the rigid class system, the *Ancien Régime*. Under this system the nobles and clergy, the privileged classes, were exempt from taxation, whilst the middle and lower classes shouldered a huge tax burden. As you might imagine, this inequity was destined to create problems. Additionally, throughout his long rule, Louis XIV engaged in a series of wars seeking to bring glory to France and to expand French borders. These wars devastated much of eastern France, resulted in the death of an estimated 20 percent of the population, and put the government into enormous debt. Louis was not unaware of the problems he and his predecessors had generated: he presciently stated on his deathbed, "After me, the deluge." Indeed, the French Revolution erupted approximately 70 years later.

# England

England, too, was a powerful European nation. Henry VIII's daughter, Elizabeth, ascended the throne in 1558 and ruled until her death in 1603. During her reign the English vanquished the mighty Spanish Armada, took an active role in the Age of Discovery, and enjoyed the talents of outstanding playwrights such as William Shakespeare and Christopher Marlowe. Elizabeth's rule set England on the path to global preeminence, a position which it held until the twentieth century. Indeed, this shrewd and intelligent monarch gave her name to the age, the Elizabethan Age.

However, following her death, the imperious policies of her successors, the Scottish-born James I and his son Charles I, led to civil war in England from 1642–1649. Some members of Parliament, mostly representatives of the growing middle class, demanded rights commensurate with their economic power and refused to be bullied by James and Charles. During a series of battles that generally pitted nobles, landed gentry, and Catholics against a strong Protestant middle-class force led by Oliver Cromwell, Cromwell and his followers emerged triumphant. After securing victory, they beheaded Charles I, an act that shocked many English. Cromwell then governed England for 10 years, a period known as the Interregnum. Although Cromwell promised a republic, he delivered a dictatorship, and shortly after his death Parliament invited Charles II, son of Charles I, to serve as monarch. Note that Charles II came at Parliament's behest and with limits placed on his royal powers.

England suffered another upheaval in the late 1600s, the Glorious Revolution. Religious tensions had contributed to the earlier civil war, and religious issues erupted again in 1688 when the monarch James II (brother of Charles II) seemed to be moving towards Catholicism. During this mostly bloodless revolution, the English made it clear that the majority of them demanded a Protestant ruler, a ruler whose powers would be limited by a Bill of Rights. Thus in 1688 Parliament invited William of Orange, a Dutch Protestant, and his wife Mary (daughter of James II), to ascend the throne of England. (James was urged to abdicate and allowed to move to France.) The next year Parliament crafted the Bill of Rights that granted rights to Parliament and citizens, and which limited the power of the monarchy. For example, under the terms of this document, the king could not suspend the laws nor could he have a standing army in peacetime without Parliament's approval. Parliament had the right to control the monarch's revenues, to meet annually and to debate freely within Parliament without fear of arrest. Furthermore, an Englishman had the right to petition the king, to have reasonable bail, and a trial by jury. By the late 1600s England was moving along a path that would lead to increased Parliamentary power, to extended voting rights for more males, and to reduced monarchical powers—i.e., the path to democracy.

## The Austrian Empire

Following their losses in the Thirty Years' War, the Austrian-based Habsburgs looked to expand their influence into lands abutting them in the south along the Danube river valley. For years these areas had been under siege from the Turks, whom the Habsburgs finally vanquished in 1683. Directing the campaigns from their beautiful city of Vienna, the Habsburgs absorbed into their holdings the non-German peoples of Lombardy (northern Italy), the Magyars of Hungary, and the Slavs and others in Bohemia (present day Czech Republic). Austria, with its vast empire and some astute leaders, was a major player in European politics for several hundred years. However, its unstable multinational empire and its failure to industrialize made Austria-Hungary, as it came to be called, a power in name only by the outbreak of World War I.

## The Holy Roman Empire

The Holy Roman Empire consisted of many German states loosely bound together and headed by an elected emperor. As we have seen, religious issues, in particular, contributed to internecine wars in the 1500s and 1600s. Near the conclusion of the Thirty Years' War, Frederick William (1640–1688), head of the state of Brandenburg-Prussia, determined to expand the influence of his family, the Hohenzollerns, and to increase Prussia's power. He consolidated his control over several of the northern German states through his highly disciplined Prussian army and an efficient bureaucracy centered in Berlin. The fine army made him a powerbroker in Central European politics and ensured that his successor, Frederick I, would be elected the Holy Roman Emperor in 1688. The Hohenzollerns maintained their power for the next two centuries, and aided by the shrewd machinations of Otto von Bismarck, became the leaders of a united Germany in 1871.

# Russia

By the mid 1600s Russia was emerging as the largest European country, albeit the least progressive. For centuries the Mongols had dominated much of Russia, but in 1480 Ivan the Great (1440–1505) defeated the Mongols from his base in Moscow and greatly expanded his holdings. He then proclaimed himself *tsar* ("Caesar") and declared that Moscow had inherited the mantle of Christian Orthodoxy subsequent to the fall of Constantinople to the Turks (1453). He made himself head of the state and the Church and used the Orthodox religion to bind his peoples together. His successors further consolidated the power of the tsar and expanded Russia's territory, but the country remained medieval; it was not until Peter the Great that a tsar sought to westernize Russia.

Peter the Great (1672–1725) was in all ways outsized: at 6'9" tall and weighing 300 pounds, he was a formidable presence with a voracious curiosity, quick intelligence, and abundant energy. His goals were to modernize Russia and to forge it into a major power. To this end, he developed Europe's largest army and fought in several wars to expand and secure Russia's borders. He made two excursions to Western Europe, bringing back technology and experts to develop industry and advance his country. He decreed the construction of a new capital, St. Petersburg—his "window on the West"—modeled on Western European cities. He ruthlessly brought nobles and peasants under his sway and forbade customs that he thought smacked of Russia's backwardness. In fact, Peter ripped beards off any aristocrat's face who dared sport a beard in court—beards were banned as "backwards"—and he had his own son executed for refusing some of his official policies! His autocratic behavior established the model for subsequent Russian rulers.

By the time of Catherine the Great, in the mid-1700s, Russia was a force in European politics. Catherine aggressively strove to enhance Russia's influence and size and also attempted to ameliorate conditions for her people through the creation of more schools, hospitals, and orphanages.

# America

Across the Atlantic in North America, sturdy English colonists were establishing towns and homesteads up and down the Eastern seaboard. The first English settlers arrived at Jamestown in 1607, and a later group landed at Plymouth in 1620. Intrepid folk, English as well as other Europeans, followed rapidly in quest of religious freedom, economic opportunity, and political autonomy.

Over time colonies emerged, quite distinct from one and other, with religion playing a major role in the founding of several colonies. English Puritans founded Massachusetts Bay Colony as a haven for their beliefs, beliefs that called for simplifying, or "purifying," Anglican Church practices. This colony was essentially a theocracy until the late 1600s, combining the interests of the state with those of strict Puritanism. Roger Williams, a religious dissenter forced out of the Bay Colony, founded Rhode Island in 1636 as a refuge for others in quest of religious freedom. Highlighting Rhode Island's commitment to toleration, the first synagogue in America was established in Newport, Rhode Island. Pennsylvania—Penn's woods—evolved from a land grant that Charles II made to William Penn, a Quaker. Penn shaped a colony that was open to all religions and peoples, and English Quakers, as well as Germans, Irish, Welsh, and other Europeans flooded in. The name of Penn's city of Philadelphia, "the city of brotherly love," expresses his philosophy. Catholics, too, had a colony of their own: Lord Baltimore established Maryland in 1634. Although most of the gentlemen settling in Maryland were Catholic, the commoners were Protestant. Therefore, very practically, religious toleration was the order of the day.

Many of the southern colonies were founded for commercial purposes, with settlers making good use of the fertile soil. The Virginia Company, an English joint-stock company (a commercial venture in which people bought shares in the hopes of earning profit) established a community at Jamestown, Virginia, in 1607, seeking vast treasure. After years of struggle, the colonists did find their treasure in the form of the tobacco plant, and Virginia grew into the wealthiest, most populous colony.

"Proprietors"—favorites of Charles II to whom he granted land—founded the Carolinas and Georgia. The Carolina proprietors envisioned colonies that would yield healthy profits from their crops; eventually, rice emerged as the most important product.

Georgia was founded for entirely different reasons. James Oglethorpe, a British general and member of Parliament, had two purposes in establishing this colony: idealistically, he desired a place where English debtors might go to start afresh; strategically, he wanted a colony that would provide a bulwark against Spanish-held Florida.

Not only were the colonies established for a variety of reasons, giving each a distinct character, but also America's topography created four regions, each possessing its own characteristics. In New England the mountainous, rocky terrain dictated small farms, readily worked by the owner and his family. Vast resources of lumber led to a flourishing ship building industry in the North. The Middle Atlantic colonies contained farms both large and small and possessed a modicum of industry. In the South the relatively flat land and rich soil led to the emergence of huge estates, which needed many hands to operate them. Slave labor seemed a necessity to plant and harvest the huge fields of tobacco, rice, and indigo. The fourth region, the frontier that stretched from north to south, was the area in which the colonists' experiences were most similar. No matter what the locale, the frontiersman had to live by his wits and his own brute strength to carve a life out of the wilderness. Yet despite these regional differences, an American identity was emerging, as we shall see in Chapter XI.

## Society in the 1600s

The seventeenth century was an especially grim period for Europeans. The many wars ravaged the countryside and destroyed prosperous cities, damaged economies, and caused widespread death. The population in Central Europe, for example, may have declined by six or seven million during this century. Additionally, the bubonic plague revisited Europe time and again, killing an estimated one million Italians, half million Spaniards, and a large percentage of Danes.[1] In England the plague struck with deadly force during the Great Plague year of 1665–1666, killing approximately 100,000 Londoners.

During this time of duress, social violence in the guise of witch hunting occurred in America and in Europe, particularly Central Europe. Generally it was marginalized individuals—the impoverished, the widowed, the emotionally dis-

1.    Anthony Esler, *The Western World: Prehistory to the Present* (Englewood Cliffs, N.J.: Prentice Hall, 1994), 457.

turbed—and very often women, who were the victims of this witch craze. State and church courts used torture to elicit confessions from the accused—confessions that led them to state that they had indeed caused death in people or livestock, had flown through the air, or had assumed the shape of an animal. It is estimated that from 1550–1700, thousands of people were executed in Switzerland and England, and many hundreds in Germany. In America, 200 people were tried in the Salem, Massachusetts witch trials and 20 of these were executed.

Historians have debated the reasons behind this witch craze. Some speculate that the underlying misogyny of Western culture contributed to the targeting of women as witches. Other historians suggest that those who were identified as witches were scapegoats, blamed for the hardships of this period. Whatever the causes, mass hysteria swept through Europe and New England during this era. By the late 1600s, however, forces of reason prevailed and the great witch craze ended.

# Overview

# The Age of Revolutions
# 1550–1900

## Revolutions and the Modern Age

A revolution suggests a dramatic change from the traditional order or from commonly held ideas. The period beginning with the Scientific Revolution around 1550, through the intellectual revolutions of the 1800s and early 1900s, was a time when age-old institutions were toppled and traditionally accepted ideas were challenged, an era when new technologies and discoveries forever altered the landscape of Western civilization. These revolutions—scientific, industrial, American, French and intellectual—moved the West into the modern age.

What do we think of as the hallmarks of modernity? Foremost is the idea, established during the Renaissance (and, of course, even earlier in Ancient Greece), that a person's life has significance and that his achievements in this world are important. During the 1600s seminal thinkers began pondering an individual's rights and his relationship to his government; they proposed that he has certain inalienable rights that it is the government's job to protect. Some concluded that the government, in fact, should reflect the will of the people and should serve the people, an idea in stark contrast to the traditional notion that people should serve the king or queen. The scientific view of the world, which has replaced, or supplemented, the religious view of the world, also characterizes the modern era: we increasingly look to science, rather than to religion, to explain the physical world. Additionally, we are connected through increased literacy and mass communications that allow us instant access to information from all parts of the globe—a far cry from the isolated villages of the Middle Ages. Further contributing to the sense of a "global village" are the advances in transportation—automobiles, trains and airplanes—that provide speedy travel to places near and far. Finally, advances in technology and the mass production of goods have created an undreamed-of abundance for the peoples of the West in the modern age.

# 10

# *The Scientific Revolution and the Enlightenment 1550–1780*

## The Scientific Revolution (1550–1700)

The Renaissance, the Reformation, and the Age of Exploration each contributed to the climate necessary for a scientific revolution to occur: the Renaissance fostered an interest in the secular world; the Reformation promoted the questioning of authority, particularly the Church's authority; and the Age of Exploration opened Europeans to a wider world, filled with different peoples and customs, that helped break their parochialism and expand their thinking. Additionally, the voyages of discovery necessitated a better understanding of natural phenomena, as well as more sophisticated technology, in order for ships to safely navigate the globe.

## Copernicus, Kepler, Galileo, and Heliocentrism

Most historians point to Nicolaus Copernicus (1473–1543) and his novel ideas regarding the movement of the earth as the starting point of the Scientific Revolution. In the early 1500s, Copernicus, through study and reasoning, concluded that the earth and planets revolved around the sun. This heliocentric (sun-centered) theory was in stark contrast to the traditional geocentric (earth-centered) theory. For over a thousand years people had believed the Church's teachings that the earth was the center of the universe, that the sun, moon and stars revolved around the earth, and that God had created man in his own image on earth. When, in the Middle Ages, scholars rediscovered the works of the ancient thinkers Aristotle and Ptolemy, who also placed the earth at the center of the universe, the Church's position seemed confirmed. How unsettling, then, to think that the world might *not* be the center of the universe! Copernicus appreciated the shocking nature of his proposition, and in fact waited until the end of his life to publish *On the Revolutions of the Heavenly Bodies* in 1543.

In the early 1600s Johannes Kepler (1571–1630), a mathematician, supported the Copernican theory by demonstrating with his calculations that the planets did, indeed, move around the sun. About the same time, the brilliant Galileo Galilei (1564–1642) challenged the Church's geocentric teachings. Galileo constructed a telescope, observed the heavens, and noted that Jupiter had four moons revolving around it—thus not everything revolved around Earth as believed. He also observed that the moon's surface was rough and uneven, not smooth and unblemished as Aristotle had proposed. Galileo published several works promoting the Copernican theory, and in 1633 the Church ultimately brought him to trial. If it allowed heretical views such as his to go unpunished, might not people start to question other aspects of Church teachings? To avoid torture, Galileo abjured his views, but remained under house arrest for the remainder of his life. (In 1992 Pope John Paul II concluded that the Church was mistaken to condemn Galileo.)

The steps taken by Copernicus, Kepler, and Galileo eventually evolved into what we call the scientific method. The scientific method involves posing a question, formulating a hypothesis, performing experiments, and analyzing the results. Reason, mathematics, and observation—the steps used by Copernicus, Kepler and Galileo in proving the heliocentric theory—are integral parts of this method.

# Newton and His Laws; Other Contributors to the Scientific Revolution

In the late 1600s, Sir Isaac Newton (1642–1727), one of the great scientific geniuses of all time, published his *Mathematical Principles of Natural Philosophy*. Newton synthesized the work of his predecessors and used his own ideas and observations to arrive at the universal law of gravitation. In essence, Newton stated that every body in the universe exerts an attraction on every other body relative to its mass and the distance between them. His brilliant law held into the twentieth century, until it was proven that subatomic particles defy this principle. Newton also did groundbreaking work in light theory and the laws of motion; additionally, he developed the branch of mathematics called calculus (as did Gottfried Leibniz, a German, about the same time).

The Scientific Revolution was a European-wide phenomenon: Copernicus was Polish, Kepler was German, Galileo was Italian, and Newton was English. Furthermore, the revolution did not focus exclusively on mathematics and physics. For example, Andreas Vesalius (1514–1564) of the Netherlands did groundbreaking work in the field of anatomy, Carl Linnaeus (1707–1778) of Sweden created the classification system for all living organisms, and William Harvey (1578–1657) of England was the first to understand the body's circulation system. Other scientists developed the microscope, the barometer, and the thermometer during this exciting period.

The Scientific Revolution paved the way for the discoveries that have continued into the twenty-first century by developing the scientific method and by providing groundbreaking work in many areas on which future generations could build. Additionally, the Scientific Revolution, with its reliance on reason and logic, fed directly into the period known as the Enlightenment.

# The Arts During the 1600s

The art of the 1600s, called Baroque, is characterized by emotional richness and technical complexity that goes beyond the realism and control of Renaissance art. Art historians suggest that the Baroque period partly reflects the reinvigoration of Catholicism during the Counter Reformation, the excitement about advances in science, and the confidence of the absolutist European states. During this period Dutchmen Rembrandt von Rijn (1606–1669) and Jan Vermeer (1632–1675), Spaniard Diego Velazquez (1599–1660), Fleming Peter Paul Rubens (1572–1640), and Italian Michelangelo Caravaggio (1571–1610) created expressive pictures with dramatic use of light and dark. The great Italian sculptor and architect Gianlorenzo Bernini (1598–1680) carved intensely passionate pieces such as *David* and the *Ecstasy of Saint Theresa*. The architecture of the period is best described as opulent, with many curves, abundant decoration, and dramatic use of space and light. The Scientific Revolution, which had led to an understanding of mathematical and engineering principles, allowed for spectacular feats of construction. Grand cathedrals such as *St. Agnese* in Rome and *St. Charles Borromaeus* in Vienna illustrate the magnificence of Baroque architecture. Finally, composers of the period such as the Germans Johann Sebastian Bach (1685–1750) and George Frederick Handel (1685–1759), likewise brought a complexity and passion to their music.

# The Enlightenment (1700–1780)

By this point in the text, it should be clear that the people of each historical period respond in some way to the events and ideas of the preceding periods. Just so, the Enlightenment thinkers of the 1700s, or *philosophes* as they are called, embraced the use of reason, so central to the discoveries of the Scientific Revolution of the 1600s. The *philosophes* believed that through reason they, too, could ascertain laws, but rather than physical laws, they sought to discover laws that governed human society, institutions, and behavior. In fact, so paramount was their belief in the power of reason that this era is often called the Age of Reason. The intellectuals of this period focused on the importance of the individual, a Renaissance ideal. Some of them sought to define a person's natural rights and to determine the type of government that would best protect these rights. Other thinkers were concerned with the general welfare of all the people. To this end, many *philosophes* sought to influence leaders who could effect positive societal changes.

Additionally, many Europeans in the 1700s were more cosmopolitan than in earlier times, thanks to the Age of Exploration, which had introduced them to new peoples and cultures. The broader vision that resulted from this contact encouraged more openness and more relativistic thinking among the educated classes. They appreciated, for example, that Christianity might not be the true religion, that perhaps religions of other cultures had equal merit.

Finally, the Enlightenment generated a great sense of optimism, for the *philosophes* believed that society was perfectible once the laws governing it were determined. This sense of optimism continued through the Enlightenment, and, some historians would contend, into the early 20th century.

# Hobbes and Locke:
# Key Pre-Enlightenment Philosophers

Before we discuss the Enlightenment, we must make note of two Englishmen, both of them seminal pre-Enlightenment thinkers whose names we still reference today when describing a particular world view; these men are Thomas Hobbes (1588–1679) and John Locke (1632–1704). Hobbes believed that in the natural state, each person's life was "solitary, poor, nasty, brutish and short." Given this fact, he argued that an absolute monarch was necessary to protect people from each other's bestial tendencies. In fact, Hobbes asserted that when people forged what he called a "social contract" with their government, they relinquished their freedom but gained much-needed order and security. Hobbes declared that even if a government failed to provide for their safety, the people had no right to rebel against it. On the other hand, John Locke believed that people were inherently good and reasonable, and because of this, Locke saw no need for a strong government. In fact, he asserted that government was best when it governed the least. Locke is sometimes called "the father of democratic theory" because he asserted that the government should be an expression of the "mutual consent of those who make up the community."[1] The government's primary role was to protect an individual's life, liberty and property, and if the government did not fulfill its job, the people had a right to rebel. Locke's ideas would later influence events in the United States and France.

## The Enlightenment Flourishes in France

The Enlightenment was centered in France where the growing, literate middle classes, as well as the upper classes, read and discussed the works of the *philosophes*. Animated conversation occurred in the hundreds of coffee houses that emerged during this period. Additionally, *salons*, held in affluent people's homes and generally orchestrated by women, brought together a wide range of intellectuals who would discourse brilliantly, it was hoped, on a variety of topics.

Although there were many important Enlightenment thinkers, Francois-Marie Arouet (1694–1778), more commonly called by his pen name Voltaire, is considered the leader of the French Enlightenment. With his sharp wit and keen intellect, he criticized the rigid class system of France and called for more personal freedoms, more tolerance, and more emphasis on reason. His calls for legal equality would prove especially influential to future events. He wrote, "Liberty consists in depending upon the laws only ... The best government seems to be that in which all ranks of men are equally protected by the laws...."[2] Additionally, Voltaire held that Christianity promoted intolerance, persecution, and fanaticism, and for this reason he rejected it. However, he did believe in a God, but his God was a rather detached essence who set the world in motion and then allowed men to go about their business as they chose. Voltaire's *Deism* (belief in God but in no affiliated religion) was influential to his own generation, as well as to subsequent ones. Finally, Voltaire corresponded with "enlightened" monarchs such as

1.    Perry, Peden and von Laue, *Sources:* I, 416.
2.    Eisen and Fuller, *The Human Adventure*: I, 206.

Frederick the Great of Prussia and Catherine the Great of Russia, exchanging ideas with them and encouraging them to put Enlightenment ideals into practice.

Jean-Jacques Rousseau (1712–1778) was another important *philosophe*. Rousseau, like Locke, believed that people were inherently good and because of this, they were able to set aside personal interest to act for the common good. He also believed that the government should reflect the "general will" of the people—a rather nebulous term that does not necessarily translate to democracy, though during his life he was hailed as the most extreme of democrats. (Napoleon and Lenin, for example, both of them autocrats, averred that they reflected "the will of the people.") Additionally, Rousseau was one of the first to put forth the notion that children should be treated as children, not as miniature adults, and in his *Emile* he proposed some revolutionary educational ideas. Finally, Rousseau promoted the use of passion and emotion, as well as reason, to lead one to "the truth," and this idea would help to inspire a later movement called Romanticism.

Another key French thinker was the Baron de Montesquieu (1689–1775), whose ideas about the separation of powers would prove influential in establishing the United States' government. Montesquieu argued that the system of checks and balances that resulted from separate legislative, executive, and judicial branches of government would prevent the rise of a strong individual or faction and would best protect the individuals' rights.

## Other Important Enlightenment Thinkers

The Enlightenment also took root in other European states, often inspiring cries to improve conditions for the downtrodden. The Italian philosopher Cesare de Beccaria (1738–1794) argued for more humane treatment of prisoners, calling for an end to torture and capital punishment. The Englishman William Wilberforce (1759–1833) decried the institution of slavery and actively campaigned to outlaw the English slave trade. And the Englishman Thomas Paine (1737–1809), who immigrated to America, penned words in his *Common Sense* of 1776 that urged Americans towards revolution: "Tis repugnant to reason, to the universal order of things, to all examples from former ages, to suppose that this Continent can long remain subject to any external power … To talk of friendship with those in whom our reason forbids us to have faith … is madness and folly."[3] The ideas of many Enlightenment thinkers would eventually translate into societal action.

---

3.    Richard D. Hefner, ed., *A Documentary History of the United States: An Expanded Edition* (New York: The New American Library, 1963), 14.

Finally, the German Immanuel Kant (1724–1804) in his *Critique of Pure Reason* contemplated the limits of reason and of human understanding, and this work is often cited as the end of the European Enlightenment.

In America the Enlightenment took a somewhat different turn: although American intellectuals enjoyed lively intellectual discourse, many held staunchly to their Christian views, never putting them aside in favor of Deism. Additionally, Americans focused on channeling intellectual inquiry towards practical purposes, such as useful inventions and discoveries.

With the concern for improving the welfare of people, we might presume that women, too, were beneficiaries of the Enlightenment. There were people like the Englishwoman Mary Wollstonecraft, as well as some men, who called for better education for women and more parity in marriage. However, the prevailing thought was that women were primarily bearers of children whose interests should focus on hearth and home; unfortunately, it would be another century before women began to experience more rights.

## The Enlightenment and Art

The arts of this period reflect the Enlightenment focus on reason, balance, and order, and thus moderated the drama and passion of the Baroque period. And because the artistic ideals of the Enlightenment were similar to those of the Ancient Greeks, we call art of this era Neoclassical. Composers such as Wolfgang Amadeus Mozart (1756–1791) and Franz Joseph Haydn (1732–1809), both Austrians, and painters like Frenchman Jacques Louis David (1748–1825) and Englishman Thomas Gainsborough (1727–1788), are prime examples of Neoclassical artists.

## Conclusion

The Enlightenment highlights the power of ideas to influence people and events. Certainly, Enlightenment ideals provided fodder for both the American and French revolutions, and, as we will see, these ideals found expression in the American *Declaration of Independence*, the United States' Constitution, and the French *Declaration of Rights of Man and Citizens*.

# 11

# *The American Revolution 1763–1783*

## An American Identity Emerges

America had continued to grow and to flourish during the 1700s with its hardy young population enjoying opportunity and freedom not found in Europe. The majority of colonists were of British descent. They spoke English, they were practicing Protestants, and they emulated the English culturally, when possible. Most regarded themselves as loyal subjects of Britain and until approximately 1760, few Americans would have predicted a rupture with Britain, no matter how disgruntled they might be with some aspects of British policy.

However, despite their cultural and historical links to Britain, the reality is that the colonists were developing a sense of independence from Britain, as well as their own identity. First, they were separated from the mother country by a 3,000-mile remove—a vast distance in any age. The physical distance alone helped to loosen the link to their homeland. Also, the type of individuals attracted to life in the New World were generally the independent sort who would, at best, have a tenuous bond to the mother country. Additionally, by 1763, fully a third of Americans were not originally British subjects—they were Germans, Scotch-Irish, Dutch, and Swedes, as well as African slaves; these groups, indeed, had little loyalty to Britain. Most important, from 1700–1775 an American national identity was evolving, which further separated the people of the New World from Britain.

Of great significance in forming this identity was the fervent religious mass movement called the Great Awakening. The Great Awakening spread across the colonies, breaking down class and geographic barriers, and uniting people through religious zeal. Benjamin Franklin's *Poor Richard's Almanac*, the second most popular book after the Bible, also helped to shape an American identity with its emphasis on thrift and hard work. Such adages as "Early to bed, early to

71

rise, make a man healthy, wealthy and wise," "God helps them that helps themselves," and "Time is money" became part of American culture. Furthermore, a strong commitment to education united the colonists and led to the establishment of many schools and colleges. The result was that by the end of the 1700s, America had the highest literacy rate in the world (for white males). Newspapers, too, played a part in forging this identity, for the colonists frequently read not only their local papers, but also those from other colonies. Additionally, the frontier experience, which was similar across geographies, helped to forge a sense of commonality among the colonists and furthered their sense of independence. Finally, each colony had a representative assembly, and colonists felt more allied to these assemblies than to a distant British Parliament. Still, despite this evolving identity, at the onset of the Revolutionary War in 1775, it is fair to note that one-third of the population supported the war, one-third was neutral, and one-third remained loyal to the British Crown, and were aptly called Loyalists.

## Tensions with Britain

The bond between the colonies and Britain was sorely tested at the conclusion of the French and Indian War in 1763. This war was a part of a larger European War, the Seven Years' War, which had proven very costly to Britain. The British Parliament's actions following this war were in large part driven by a desire to defray some of its enormous debt. It imposed a series of taxes on imports to America—on sugar, paper, paint, and playing cards, for example—that inflamed many colonists. They were willing to pay taxes imposed by their local assemblies, but they were aggrieved at being taxed by a distant Parliament in which they had no representation. Furthermore, the British government maintained an army of 7,000 men in America at the conclusion of this war, allegedly to protect the colonists from Indians. In many colonists' eyes, however, this seemed more like an army of occupation, an army that they were forced to house and feed under the terms of the Quartering Act. The Boston Massacre of 1770, in which some British soldiers—bullied and harassed by a Boston mob—fired and killed five men, was additional proof, militants proclaimed, that they were enduring an army of occupation. Finally, in 1773 the tax on tea drove Sam Adams and other Bostonians to engage in a "tea party," in which they dumped 343 chests of tea into Boston Harbor. Parliament's response was severe: Boston was put under strict military control of the Crown by the terms of the Intolerable Acts.

# The American War of Revolution (1775–1783)

These issues and events fueled the anger of many colonials, which they fanned through widely disseminated essays, letters, and newspapers. The First Continental Congress, held in 1774, assembled 51 men such as George Washington, Benjamin Franklin, and John Adams to assert colonial rights to Parliament. Then, in 1775, British soldiers, marching to Concord, Massachusetts in order to seize suspected rebel supplies, were fired upon at Lexington—the so-called "shot heard round the world"—and were later routed at Concord; thus began the War of Revolution.

An observer at the outset of the war might have speculated about its eventual outcome. How could the motley group of poorly trained and abysmally equipped Americans defeat one of the finest militaries in the world? Britain possessed not only experienced soldiers, but also the world's finest navy and a strong industrial base; additionally, thousands of Hessian (German) mercenaries supplemented its forces. To their advantage, the rebels had the great leadership of George Washington, knowledge of their terrain, and a strong commitment to their cause.

Tom Paine's *Common Sense* of 1776 inspired many to take up arms. He urged: "O! ye that love mankind! Ye that dare oppose not only the tyranny but the tyrant, stand forth! Every spot of the old world is overrun with oppression. Freedom hath been hunted round the Globe ... Receive the fugitive, and prepare in time an asylum for mankind!"[1]

Additionally, the French helped the rebel cause: they covertly sent supplies to the rebels at the outset of the war and eventually supported them overtly with men and ships, both of which proved essential to the ultimate British defeat at Yorktown.

The revolution quickly evolved into a war of independence and this was made manifest on July 4, 1776, when the Americans proclaimed The Declaration of Independence. Developed by a committee of five, written by Thomas Jefferson (and echoing John Locke), this seminal document espoused:

> We hold these truths to be self-evident, that all men are created equal, that they are endowed by their Creator with certain inalienable rights ... life, liberty, and the pursuit of happiness. That to secure these rights, governments are instituted among men ... That whenever any form of government becomes destructive of these ends, it is the right of the people to alter or to abolish it.... [2]

1.    Hefner, *A Documentary History*, 15.
2.    Ibid., 15.

Besides asserting these unassailable rights, the document also offered justification on many grounds for the "united states of America" to separate from Britain.

The Revolutionary War lasted six years, from 1775–1781. The year 1777 was an especially critical one and illustrates both the highs and lows of this conflict. In the summer of 1777, the Americans won a stunning victory at Saratoga, capturing over one-quarter of the British army in America. Their victory led to active French engagement in the Revolutionary War, and by mid-1778 the French commander Comte de Rochambeau arrived with 6,000 troops to support the Americans. Additionally, the French navy began harrying the British fleet, attempting to cut off supply lines. However, late 1777 and early 1778 found the Continental army wintering at Valley Forge, the men's morale flagging from several recent defeats and with hunger, cold, and disease afflicting them. Over 2,500 perished; Valley Forge, the low point of the war, was a true test of colonial grit.

The military engagements slowly moved from the North to the South; British strategists had decided that the mostly untouched South, with a fair share of Loyalists, might prove a more effective base from which to launch a new campaign in 1780. Initially victorious, in 1781 the British found themselves wedged between the French fleet and colonial and French forces at Yorktown, Virginia. British General Charles Cornwallis tendered his sword; the Revolutionary War was at an end.

# The War's Conclusion: The United States of America

The results of the American Revolution were manifold. The three American diplomats charged with negotiating a settlement with Britain—John Adams, John Jay, and Benjamin Franklin—emerged in 1783 with a peace treaty favorable to America: Britain recognized the independence of the United States and ceded it all of its territory east of the Mississippi River, from the border of Canada in the north and to the border of Florida in the south. (Spain controlled Florida, the navigation rights to the Mississippi River, and the land west of the Mississippi. The United States obtained Florida from Spain in 1823; France briefly gained control of Spain's Mississippi and western holdings, but sold this vast territory to the United States in 1803.) Over 60,000 Loyalists left the country, some emigrating to Canada, and a few returning to England. Republican fervor also gripped the states, and property requirements were lowered in many areas to allow for more representative government. As the nation pushed west, settlers were allowed full representation in their state assemblies. And with the declaration that "all men are created equal" several states, particularly in the North, began to abolish the institution of slavery. Although some Southern slaveholders like James Madison and George Washington would eventually free their slaves, the Southern economy was too dependent on slave labor for most others to follow their example. Finally, the American Revolution with its positive outcome was inspirational to other nations seeking more representative government. Indeed, in less than a decade, France would have its own revolution.

Now that they had gained their independence, American leaders were faced with the challenge of forging a viable government. During the war the colonies had operated under the Articles of the Confederation, a document that had established a weak federal government. Unable to collect taxes or to raise an army, it "requisitioned" money and men from the states, hoping that each would fulfill its obligations. Following the war, the states jealously guarded their autonomy, not wanting to cede too much power to a central government. Chaos reigned as states imposed tariffs on each other, printed their own money, and negotiated with foreign powers. By the mid 1780s, it became clear to the men called the founding fathers that a stronger central government was necessary if a United States of America was to operate effectively as a nation.

The United States was blessed to have at this moment a group of men who embraced the Enlightenment ideal of working for the common good and who would set aside personal ambitions to achieve this goal—men like George Washington, Benjamin Franklin, James Madison, and Alexander Hamilton. (Thomas Jefferson and John Adams were in Europe, serving their country in other capacities.) In May of 1787, they and 51 other delegates met in Philadelphia to hammer out a constitution that would establish a more powerful central government, yet would balance states' rights against the power of the federal government. With a nod to Montesquieu, they also sought to create a system of checks and balances among the three branches of government—the executive, judicial and legislative—such that none would become too powerful. With the guiding force of James Madison who favored a strong central government, and with much debate and compromise, these men completed their task in September of the same year. In the last months of 1787 and throughout 1788, all the states save North Carolina and Rhode Island ratified the Constitution and it became the law of the land. A few years later Madison and several others developed a Bill of Rights, which clearly delineated the personal freedoms that Americans would enjoy; the states ratified these first 10 amendments to the Constitution in 1791.

The country was also blessed to have George Washington, "His Excellency" as he was called, serve as its first president. Towering over most of his contemporaries at 6'3", he was the most admired man in America: he had selflessly and tire-lessly served his country during the Revolution, and although he fervently wanted to live out his postwar days at Mt. Vernon, he responded to the call to preside over the Constitutional Convention and to serve as America's first president. Although neither the most brilliant nor the best educated of the founding fathers, his integrity, dignity, and courage made him the only choice for president. Washington served two terms in office, establishing many of the precedents that set the United States' presidency on a clear course over subsequent centuries.

The new government confronted many tests, but in the most general of terms, its mission was to establish itself as a force both nationally and internationally. We will see how it fared in Chapter XIV.

# 12

# *The French Revolution 1789–1815*

The French Revolution remains one of the most significant and inspirational events of European history. Many of the participants in this revolution drew on Enlightenment ideals as they sought to implement "*liberté, égalité, fraternité*" (liberty, equality, fraternity) in French society—ideals of personal freedoms and representative government, of legal equality and equal opportunity, and of nationalism. Other participants, of course, sought to improve their socioeconomic position and to rectify age-old injustices. The ripple effects of this revolution influenced Europe throughout the 1800s and gave rise to many powerful ideas and movements that continue to shape the world today.

## Causes of the French Revolution

As we discussed in Chapter IX, there were many deeply entrenched problems in French society and by the late 1700s conditions were ripe for revolution. There were several causes of this revolution, and among the most important was the rigid class system, the *Ancien Régime*, which afforded many privileges and much power to the clergy (the First Estate) and to the nobles (the Second Estate) and generally deprived privilege and power to the rest of society (the Third Estate, 98 percent of the population). In all fairness we should acknowledge that some clergy and nobles, imbued with Enlightenment ideals, identified with the aims of the Third Estate.

Within the vast Third Estate, each group had specific grievances. The largest group, comprising 80 percent of the French population, was the peasants, who wanted more land, as well as relief from their enormous tax burden and their obligations to the local lord. The urban workers (the proletariat, as they are sometimes called) desired more jobs, less taxation, and cheaper food. They constituted

500,000 of the 600,000 inhabitants of Paris in 1789 and were the Revolution's most incendiary force. The middle class (the bourgeoisie) called for more freedoms, less taxes and more political opportunity commensurate with its growing wealth. In the true Enlightenment spirit, many Frenchmen criticized the structure of their government and society, and called for the implementation of equality and liberty. While some of the bourgeoisie envisioned France as a constitutional monarchy, others desired a more radical change, a republic on the American model.

Another cause of the French Revolution was the weak leadership of Louis XVI, who preferred to spend his time hunting and tinkering with clocks rather than in administering his government. His marriage to Marie Antoinette added to his unpopularity. Marie was a princess from Austria, a traditional enemy of France, and, although charming, she was a frivolous woman as well as a spendthrift. In fact, in one year she incurred the equivalent of $1.5 million in gambling debts.[1]

A financial crisis set the revolution in motion. Louis XVI needed more money to run the country: the wars of his predecessors, the maintenance of the army, and his opulent lifestyle had created enormous debt. The solution, of course, was to tax the privileged classes, but the clergy and the nobles resisted this measure. Desperate, Louis called for a meeting at Versailles of the Estates General, a representative assembly of the three Estates. This was the first convocation of the Estates General in over 175 years, and highlights Louis' urgent desire to effect financial reform.

## The Early Years

The meeting in May 1789 was filled with strife, but eventually some clergy and nobles joined the Third Estate to form what they called the National Assembly. As an assembly they asserted that they spoke for all of France and vowed not to disband until they had implemented major changes. Eventually Louis ordered all the members of the first two Estates to join the National Assembly, hoping that he would get the financial reform that he desperately needed.

Meanwhile, in Paris, the urban workers were in a surly mood: they blamed the government for elevated food prices following a poor harvest and for widespread unemployment. On July 14th 1789, a mob attacked the Bastille prison, a symbol

---

1.    Roger Beck et al., *Modern World History: Patterns of Interaction* (Evanston: McDougal Littell, 2001), 195.

of royal power in which political prisoners had traditionally been incarcerated. When the mob attacked the Bastille, many of the guards participated, for they, too, were part of the disenfranchised. The rioters eventually killed the governor of the Bastille and the mayor of Paris, cutting off their heads and parading them through the streets of Paris on pikes. The fall of the Bastille was highly symbolic and is celebrated today in France as the day of national liberation from the shackles of the absolutist monarchy. July 14$^{th}$ is thus the French equivalent of the American July 4$^{th}$.

The spirit of rebellion spread to the countryside, and in August the Great Fear swept over rural France. Peasants broke into local estates, killed nobles, looted property, and burned papers tying them to their feudal obligations. Through force, they hoped to destroy the Old Regime.

Meanwhile, in Versailles, the National Assembly made some revolutionary changes. Unsettled by events in the countryside, the aristocracy rescinded its traditional rights and announced the end of feudalism in the August Decrees. The decrees granted the peasants more land as well as the tax relief they had demanded. (From this point on most of the peasantry was a conservative force in the revolution—they had gotten what they wanted, so why agitate any further?) With the publication of the August Decrees, many aristocrats fled France and many of these émigrés, as they came to be called, continued to work against the revolution from their bases in other European countries.

That August the National Assembly also issued the Declaration of the Rights of Man and Citizen, a seminal document like the American Declaration of Independence, filled with Enlightenment ideals. For example:

I.     Men are born ... free, and equal in respect of their rights.

II.    The end of all political associations is the preservation of the natural ... rights of man; and these rights are liberty, property, security and resistance of oppression.

III.   The law is an expression of the will of the community.

IV.    No man ought to be molested on account of his opinions, not even on account of his religious opinions.... [2]

---

2.     Marvin Perry, Joseph R. Peden, Theodore H. von Laue, *Sources of the Western Tradition*, 5$^{th}$ edition, vol. II (Boston: Houghton Mifflin, 2003), 106–107.

Finally, in this first great year of the Revolution, the working-class women of Paris took action in October, marching to Versailles and demanding that Louis and his queen return to Paris where they could remain under closer scrutiny. Under pressure from the 10,000 women, Louis and his family succumbed to their demand and returned to Paris.

In the next two years the Assembly reorganized France and hammered out a constitution. This Constitution of 1791 was a remarkably moderate document in many ways, retaining Louis XVI as the monarch, albeit one limited in his powers. The document also called for a Legislative Assembly, elected by men who were tax payers and property owners, i.e., about half of the male population. The Church was brought under state control, with clergymen receiving their salaries from the state.

Many factions within France, however, were unhappy with the constitution. A radical group called the Jacobins demanded universal male suffrage and the elimination of the monarchy. Some women, like Olympe de Gouges, demanded political rights for women. Other highly nationalistic groups wanted to export the revolution to the rest of Europe. And the royal family, hoping to join the other émigrés, attempted to flee France; the family was caught at the border and Louis, his queen, and their son remained prisoners from this time onward.

## The Revolution Intensifies

During the next several years the situation grew increasingly violent. Within France, the Jacobins, with mastermind Maximilien Robespierre at their head, gained control of the government and instituted the Reign of Terror, which lasted from 1793 into 1794. Robespierre wanted to create a "republic of virtue"; to this end thousands were identified as enemies of the state and executed. Although historians debate the actual number killed during the Reign of Terror, 40,000 victims seems a reasonable estimate. Enemies of the revolution were executed by guillotine, the modern, "enlightened" instrument of death designed to provide a quick, more humane exit from this world. Among those guillotined were Louis XVI and Marie Antoinette, both of whom were executed in 1793. Robespierre also outlawed the Catholic Church, and drawing on the Enlightenment idea of Deism, declared the "worship of the Supreme Being" as the only state religion. In July of 1794, this violent phase of the revolution devoured Robespierre himself, and in reaction, a calmer political period began in 1795.

Meanwhile, beginning in 1792 France waged war against Prussia and Austria, and later, Britain, Spain, and the Netherlands. French soldiers were filled with zeal as they fought to spread *liberté, égalité* and *fraternité;* the army swelled to 800,000 men, the largest European army to this point in history, and commanders of talent, not royal birth, led the French to multiple victories. It was at this point that the *Marseillaise,* that patriotic song from the south of France, became the national anthem of all the French.

# Napoleon Bonaparte and the French Empire

During this period Napoleon Bonaparte (1769–1821) entered the stage of history. As we consider Napoleon, it is worth contemplating the age-old question, "Does the man shape the times or do the times shape the man?" Certainly Napoleon was a man of genius, possessing a keen memory, excellent administrative skills, and rapid, astute decision-making ability. He brought a sense of his own destiny to all that he undertook, and acted with energy and determination. He organized and modernized France, establishing many key institutions that exist today. As he conquered Europe, he spread and implemented many Revolutionary ideals, altering Europe permanently. Yet, if Corsica had not become a French possession shortly before his birth in 1769 (it had belonged to Italy), he would not have had the advantage of attending a French military school or of fighting for France in the revolution. Nor, in an earlier period in history when lineage, not talent, was the determining factor in ascension through the ranks, would he have had the opportunity to rise so rapidly to power. So, as with most cases of the "great people" of history, we must conclude that it is the confluence of individual talent and events that allow a person to leave his mark on history.

In 1799 Napoleon, a young, popular, and talented general, seized control of the French government. The government had evolved into an unpopular oligarchy run by and for the bourgeoisie. Most French welcomed the leadership of this forceful man-of-action who promised some stability after the upheavals of the past ten years. Napoleon initially took the title of "First Consul"—a nod to the Roman republic—but in 1804 he asked the people to approve the title of Emperor, which they did overwhelmingly.

Upon assuming power, Napoleon brought much vigor to organizing France, abolishing anything that smacked of feudalism, and opening careers in government to men of talent. He established a national Bank of France to help stabilize and regulate the economy and mandated that taxes should be collected in a fair and orderly manner. He created a national Board of Education to standardize education and established schools for boys of promise. The Concordat that Napoleon forged with the Catholic Church in 1801 was beneficial to the Church and to him: this agreement reestablished the supremacy of the Catholic Church in France, but placed all clergy under state control. Additionally, by signing the Concordat, the pope legitimized Napoleon's rule. Perhaps most significantly, he codified the laws; his Napoleonic codes guaranteed equality under the law, the right to private property, and certain personal liberties, such as freedom of religion. However, despite these reforms, Napoleon did not allow freedom of speech or of the press; indeed, he practiced censorship and utilized spies and secret police to ferret out detractors.

Napoleon focused most of his energy on France during the first five years of his rule, but in 1804 he decided it was time to build a European empire. He recognized that powerful and wealthy Britain, protected by the Channel, was a prime opponent and he spent considerable time devising a strategy to invade England. However, in 1805 at the Battle of Trafalgar, Lord Horatio Nelson and the British navy soundly defeated half the French fleet. Napoleon relinquished the dream of an imminent invasion, but he eventually sought to threaten Britain economically by cutting off its trade with Europe through a policy called the Continental Plan.

After the dismal Battle of Trafalgar, Napoleon focused on subduing continental Europe, utilizing his army as the means to victory. And victories he had! By 1810 Napoleon had mastered Europe, and his Grand Empire encompassed all the continent except the Balkans. He placed his siblings on the thrones of several regions, for who would prove more loyal than family? Napoleon sought to reform the areas under his control, destroying any remnants of feudalism and instituting the Code Napoleon to spread the idea of civic equality. Most historians believe that he was driven by an idea of a unified Europe, brought together by uniform, rational, enlightened law—with himself as emperor of all.

## Napoleon's Defeat and the Congress of Vienna

In 1812, however, Napoleon made a great misjudgment when he decided to invade Russia; it had not complied with his Continental Plan and had continued to trade with Britain. He invaded Russia with a force of 600,000 men comprised of soldiers from all parts of his realm, but with supplies for just three weeks. He intended the campaign to be a short one, and planned to supplement his rations by living off the Russian soil. The Russians, however, retreated as Napoleon advanced, burning their fields and slaughtering their livestock. When Napoleon's starving troops reached Moscow, they found that the Russians had burned this city, too, offering them no refuge from the onset of an early winter. The Russian emperor refused to negotiate with Napoleon, and Napoleon was forced to retreat, fearful of being trapped in Moscow during the long, harsh Russian winter. Most of his army perished from starvation, sickness, and exposure, and he was left with fewer than 100,000 men when he returned to France.

The powers of Europe recognized that this was the moment to strike! In 1813, the Grand Alliance smashed Napoleon and his newly raised, under-trained army at the Battle of the Nations. To insure that Napoleon would not mount a counteroffensive, the victors sent Napoleon to Elba, a small island off the coast of Italy. Napoleon made one last, valiant effort to regain his power in 1815, returning for the Hundred Days to challenge the united powers of Europe. He was soundly defeated at the Battle of Waterloo and exiled to St. Helena, an island far from Europe in the south Atlantic, where he died in 1821.

Following Napoleon's defeat in 1813, the great powers of Europe met in Vienna during 1814–1815 to reorganize the continent and to ensure stability following the years of war and French domination. The Austrian Klemens von Metternich dominated the Congress of Vienna, but representatives from Britain, Prussia, Russia, and France—yes, even France—were key players. Metternich sought to achieve a balance of power in Europe, with no country too powerful. He also sought to restore the traditional ruling families to their thrones and to compensate those countries that had suffered under the French yoke, as well as those that had helped to defeat the emperor.

The Congress of Vienna was successful in that it did prevent a European-wide war for a century, until World War I engulfed the continent. However, Metternich and the other diplomats failed to recognize—or chose to ignore—the powerful ideas ignited by the French Revolution. Many European peoples were no longer content to live under a monarchy and demanded a more representative government that ensured greater personal freedoms. In subsequent years rebellions took place in countries such as France, Austria, and Russia on behalf of this notion of liberalism. Napoleon had also unleashed powerful nationalistic sentiment as he marched through Europe: many people recognized that they were Belgian, or German, or Italian and did want to be a part of France, or of any other country. Thus, the three aforementioned peoples fought wars to establish their nationhood in the ensuing decades, and the independent countries of Belgium, Germany and Italy had emerged by 1871. Indeed, the nationalism unleashed by the French Revolution would have profound effects that endure even in today's world.

# 13

# *The Industrial Revolution 1760–1830*

Along with the French Revolution, the Industrial Revolution had a dramatic impact on Europe and eventually the rest of the world. Sometimes historians refer to these two events as the "dual revolutions" because they occurred at approximately the same time and because they had such an enormous effect in propelling the globe into the modern era. Just as the French Revolution illustrates the power of Enlightenment ideas, so the Industrial Revolution manifests the practical face of the Scientific Revolution when science was applied to industry.

## Britain Industrializes

The Industrial Revolution began in Great Britain around 1760 for a host of reasons. First, an Agricultural Revolution had occurred in Britain in the early 1700s. Farming had become more scientific (thanks to the influence of the Scientific Revolution) as the wealthy landed gentry experimented with new kinds of fertilizers and developed hardier strains of crops and livestock. The results of their experimentation were bumper harvests and healthier stock. Additionally, these wealthy landowners employed innovative machinery and enclosed sizeable tracts of land to work the soil more efficiently. As a consequence, they no longer needed large numbers of tenant farmers or day laborers to tend their fields. These unemployed rural workers provided a ready source of manpower for the new factories. Britain also possessed natural resources to fuel the Industrial Revolution. It had an abundance of iron and coal deposits, as well as rivers, canals, and many harbors along its coastline to facilitate transport. Moreover, its colonial empire provided raw materials for factories and a ready market in which to sell manufactured goods.

Furthermore, the British government sought to nurture economic development. It actively supported entrepreneurs, offering patents to protect inventions and prizes for new technology. The government had established a Bank of England in 1694, which helped to stabilize the economy, and had created a stock exchange in 1773, which allowed the wealthier classes to invest in new businesses and to share in their profits. It embraced Adam Smith's ideas, put forth in 1776 in *The Wealth of Nations*. Smith, often called the father of capitalism, believed in a laissez-faire economy, i.e., one in which the government does not intrude, thus allowing the natural laws of supply and demand to prevail. Smith believed that as each individual pursued his own economic self-interest, all of society would benefit and prosper.

Finally, we should note that Britain was spared invasion during the Napoleonic wars, and the Industrial Revolution developed freely, without the upheavals that shook the continent. It was not until after 1815, when stability returned to continental Europe, that the Industrial Revolution took hold there.

The Industrial Revolution occurred first in Britain's textile industry. Inventions such as the spinning jenny (1764) produced more thread, Richard Arkwright's water frame (1769) wove finer, stronger thread, and American Eli Whitney's cotton gin (1793) made more raw cotton readily available. Arkwright's frames were so enormous that he had to construct large buildings in which to accommodate them—the first factories. Arkwright initially relied on water to power his frames, but later introduced the steam engine.

The steam engine, perfected and sold by James Watt in 1776, is considered the major breakthrough of the Industrial Revolution. With the steam engine Britain possessed a moveable source of power, and factories no longer needed to be placed by water. Many factories developed near the coal deposits of the English Midlands since coal provided the energy source. Eventually, Watt's steam engine led to the creation of the railroad, which greatly facilitated trade within Britain, leading to cheaper transportation costs and less expensive goods. The railroad also served to unify the nation since people could travel swiftly and cheaply to most parts of their country.

# Effects of the Industrial Revolution in Britain

There were, of course, many positive effects of the Industrial Revolution. In general terms, Britain became wealthier as a nation and its citizens enjoyed a better standard of living: the Industrial Revolution allowed for plentiful and cheaper goods, often leading to improved health. (As a minor example, more people could now afford cotton underwear—a necessity for better hygiene.) Burgeoning factories provided steady employment for workers, who no longer had to labor in the fields according to nature's rhythms and whims. The revolution increased the size of the middle class, rewarding those who were inventive and entrepreneurial, and class lines often blurred as business magnates rubbed shoulders with the aristocracy. Finally, factory life afforded working class men and women the opportunity to establish bonds that led to the development of powerful labor unions and to a fledgling feminist movement.

The Industrial Revolution also produced many negative results, especially at its outset. People poured into the new factory towns and lived in dirty and overcrowded buildings. The factories themselves were often perilous places to work, with no safety regulations and with unsanitary and dangerous working conditions the norm. An overabundance of willing workers meant that they were often exploited, and wages were low and hours long. Generally both mother and father had to work to support the family, and they often brought their young children along, too, for small and nimble fingers were capable of performing some factory tasks. These children never attended school, never had the benefits of fresh air. Additionally, the factories and their wastes blighted the countryside.

Over the course of the 1800s, the British government sought to address some of the negative effects of the Industrial Revolution. As early as 1802 the government passed legislation limiting the hours that children could work, and a more comprehensive Factory Act in 1833 further limited child labor. During the latter part of the 19th century, prime ministers William Gladstone and Benjamin Disraeli enacted legislation that called for better housing, safer and cleaner factories, and mandatory public education for children. Additionally, although the British government initially banned labor unions, it rescinded the ban in 1824, which allowed workers to make their voices heard through bargaining, picketing, and strikes. And, throughout the 1800s, the government extended the franchise to greater numbers of British men, making them feel a part of the system.

# The Industrial Revolution Spreads

Although we have focused on Britain in this chapter, a similar pattern of industrialization occurred on the continent at the conclusion of the Napoleonic wars in 1815. Factory workers were initially subjected to harsh living and working conditions, which improved over time through government intervention. Belgium and the German states were among the first areas to industrialize, and in fact, by 1900, Germany was one of the world's most industrialized nations. For a host of reasons, France did not industrialize until after 1850, and Russia and other areas of Central and Eastern Europe did not begin to industrialize until the end of the century.

Across the Atlantic, the United States embraced the new technology. Samuel Slater, an English immigrant, built the first factory in Pawtucket, Rhode Island in 1783, and more factories, then railroad lines, followed. The United States also boasted a host of talented inventors: in 1807 Robert Fulton developed the steam ship, in 1834 Cyrus McCormick produced a mechanized reaper, and in 1837 Samuel F.B. Morse invented the telegraph.

The Industrial Revolution continued in a second major wave in Europe, the United States, and Japan after 1850. During this period the German Gottlieb Daimler developed the internal combustion engine, and another German, Rudolf Diesel, perfected the diesel engine. In the United States, Thomas Edison created the electric light bulb and a more powerful electric generator. And in 1876, Alexander Graham Bell, who had emigrated from Scotland to America, invented the first telephone.

# New Ideas and Movements: Marxism and Romanticism

The Industrial Revolution provoked much reflection and prompted new philosophies. One of the most significant thinkers to emerge during this period—indeed one of the most influential men of the modern age—was Karl Marx (1818–1883), co-author of *The Communist Manifesto* (1848). Marx was born into a non-practicing Jewish family in Germany and led a peripatetic life, finally settling with his wife and children in England. Marx came to believe that "The history of all hitherto existing society is the history of class struggle."[1] He asserted that in modern times the ruthless, exploitative capitalistic system accounted for class oppression, and urged the workers (the proletariat) to unite and overthrow their factory-owner masters (the bourgeoisie). The *Manifesto*'s concluding phrase, "Workers of the world, unite!" was a call to arms that echoed—and continues to echo—down the corridors of time, heard by Lenin, Mao, Castro, and countless others. Marx also disavowed Christianity, deeming it the "opiate of the masses": Christianity, with its focus on a glorious afterlife, prevented the working classes from rebelling against the oppression in their daily lives.

---

1.    Perry, Peden, von Laue, *Sources*, II: 184.

The dual revolutions also led to the cultural movement called Romanticism. Romantics glorified nature in response to the factories' desecration of the countryside. As Englishman William Wordsworth (1770–1850) declared in his *Tintern Abby*, "… Nature never did betray/The heart that loved her; tis her privilege,/To lead from joy to joy…." [2] The Romantics reacted against the Enlightenment emphasis on reason and science; rather, they celebrated passion as leading to "the truth." They also extolled the man of action and genius, like Napoleon, who rises above the pack to shape his own destiny. Finally, Romantics were fascinated with foreign lands and exotic places.

Romanticism was widespread and included English poets William Wordsworth, Percy Bysshe Shelley (1792–1822), and John Keats (1795–1821); German writer Wolfgang von Goethe (1749–1832); Polish composer Frederic Chopin (1810–1849), German composer Richard Wagner (1813–1883), and Russian composer Pyotr Tchaikovsky (1840–1893). The music of one of the world's foremost composers, Ludwig von Beethoven (1770–1827), represents the transition from the Classical to the Romantic period. Romanticism also found expression in art; prime examples are painters Englishman William Turner (1775–1851) and Frenchman Eugene Delacroix (1798–1863). The works of each of these individuals illustrates the deep emotion so central to Romanticism.

# Conclusion

The Industrial Revolution forever changed the economic, social, and political landscape of Europe and the world. Today we reap the benefits of this revolution with an abundance of goods and a host of technological innovations unimaginable to earlier generations. Western society possesses a vast and flourishing middle class, as well as a working class that enjoys certain safety nets provided by the government. However, it is also evident that the blessings of this movement have come with a cost to the West: hurried and sometimes isolated lives, a threatened environment, and a voracious appetite for the world's finite resources.

---

2.    Reuben A. Brower, Anne D. Ferry, and David Kalstone, *Beginning with Poems: An Anthology* (New York: W.W. Norton and Company, Inc., 1966), 205.

# 14

# *The United States in the 1800s:*
# *From Revolution to Evolution*

In the nineteenth century the United States confronted many challenges as it wrestled with the reality of self-governance. First and foremost, the newly created government had to define its role both domestically and internationally. Additionally, the push westward and the desire to acquire more land generated problems: confrontations with foreign powers, conflict with Native Americans, and questions about how the new territory should be incorporated into the United States. The divisive issue of slavery culminated mid-century in the bloodbath of the Civil War and posed the challenge: would the United States be irrevocably sundered? As the century progressed, millions of immigrants poured into America, testing the country's ability to absorb them and to retain its American identity. Toward the end of the 1800s, industrialization created vast wealth for some and exploitation of others and promoted rapid urbanization with its attendant problems; the effects of industrialization became a major challenge to the United States.

## Establishing the New Government: Challenges at Home

The Constitution had established a strong federal government while simultaneously preserving some states' rights. How would this arrangement operate in actuality? When George Washington assumed the presidency in 1789 his two most important advisors had starkly different perspectives on the role of the central government: Alexander Hamilton, the secretary of the Treasury, envisioned a vigorous federal government that would flex its muscles to bind the country together. On the other hand, Thomas Jefferson, secretary of State, desired a restricted federal government and more autonomy for the states. Throughout his two terms of office, Washington listened carefully to their advice then did what he thought best for the country. Most often he embraced Hamilton's ideas, for Hamilton persuasively argued that the Constitution gave the federal government implied powers through its "necessary and proper" clause, often called the "elastic" clause because it expands the government's power. (People that endorsed—and continue to endorse—Hamilton's interpretation of this clause are called "loose constructionists," and those that adhere to a stricter interpretation of this clause are deemed "strict constructionists.") This argument led Washington to support the creation of the Bank of the United States, a national bank that would help stabilize the economy. And Washington himself led a force to quell an uprising of Pennsylvania whiskey-makers who resented paying a federal tax on their whiskey; he made it clear that the national government would use force to implement its laws.

Even though Washington established many precedents for his successors, they nonetheless continued to wrestle with the issue of federal power. Sometimes events prompted presidents to act practically rather than philosophically. For example, Thomas Jefferson, who became president in 1800 and who planned to reduce the cost and size of the federal government, greatly expanded the power of the government when he purchased the Louisiana Territory from France in 1803; it was a vast stretch of land offered at a cheap price, an opportunity impossible to pass up. Jefferson, a strict constructionist, admitted he had "stretched the Constitution until it cracked."[1] Sometimes philosophy trumped practicality, as when President Andrew Jackson, the "peoples' president," refused to renew the charter of the Second Bank of the United States in 1833. Jackson—a strict constructionist—believed that the bank was illegal, elitist, and monopolistic. His controversial destruction of the Bank, however, led to economic chaos for 10 years.

The Supreme Court also helped to define the role of the national government during the first part of the 1800s. The great Supreme Court Chief Justice, John Marshall, who served from 1801–1835, is credited with making the Supreme Court a co-equal with the other branches of government. Marshall oversaw at least 50 cases that dealt with numerous constitutional issues; two of his most important cases are *Marbury vs. Madison* (1803), in which the Court ruled that it had the right to review any Congressional or state law; and *McCulloch vs. Maryland* (1819), in which the court decreed that the federal government prevails over the state when the two are in conflict.

---

1.    Allan Nevins and Henry Steele Commager, *A Pocket History of the United States* (New York: Washington Square Press, 1981), 136.

The members of Congress, too, wrangled over the power of the national government, especially with respect to Congress's role in the economy. By 1840 two political parties had emerged: the Democrats, dedicated to reducing the power of the central government, and the Whigs, who believed in a vigorous central government. Democrats attracted workers and small farmers, while the Whigs attracted industrialists and larger farmers.

## Establishing the New Government: Challenges Abroad

During this same period the United States also needed to define its role internationally. Washington had sought to keep the fledgling nation out of foreign affairs, and in his Farewell Address urged his countrymen to abjure long-lasting alliances with other nations: "It is our true policy to steer clear of permanent alliances, with any portion of the foreign world" he declared.[2] Washington and the subsequent two presidents, John Adams and Thomas Jefferson, used diplomacy and trade embargoes to prevent American entanglement in European affairs. (Jefferson did send a small fleet to subdue the Barbary pirates—raiders from the Barbary States of North Africa—who had long disrupted commercial shipping.) But in 1812, President James Madison, encouraged by a faction known as the War Hawks, asked Congress to declare war on Britain, which it did. The British had repeatedly interfered with American shipping, had forcibly impressed American sailors into their navy, and, the War Hawks argued, had encouraged Indian uprisings to deter Americans from moving west. Although the British invaded the new capital, Washington D.C., and burned the Capitol building and White House, neither side had won the war when it concluded in 1814. However, the war served to unify America and to generate an increased nationalism and self-confidence. Later, in 1823, President James Monroe articulated the Monroe Doctrine, which warned Europe against establishing any additional colonies in the New World or interfering in the affairs of this region.

During the remainder of the 1800s there were conflicts with Native Americans and with Mexico, but generally the United States remained free of entanglements with foreign powers until the Spanish-American war of 1898. The United States engaged in this war to support Cuban rebels protesting Spain's harsh policies, for Spain had long governed its colony of Cuba with a heavy hand. In 1898 Cubans revolted against this oppression and the United States came to the rebels'

---

2.    Hefner, *A Documentary History*, 66.

aid. In truth, economic self-interest primarily prompted America's entry into the rebellion: the uprising in Cuba threatened to wreak havoc on the American economy since the United States had significant investments in Cuba as well as important trade relations with it. The war was brief: the United States defeated the Spanish in Cuba, in Puerto Rico, and the Philippines. As a consequence of the war, Cuba was declared an independent republic, and the United States gained the Philippines and Puerto Rico.

# The Lure of the West: Manifest Destiny

The attraction of vast and fertile land, great mineral resources, and immense forests drew Americans to the West. Farmers, prospectors, trappers—and later doctors, lawyers, merchants—ventured forth with the belief that through hard work, and a bit of luck, a bright future awaited them. With the press westward, the notion of Manifest Destiny took hold—the belief that it was the United States' right to control the whole of North America.

As pioneers pushed beyond the Mississippi River in the 1830s and 1840s, their movement brought the United States into confrontation with Britain, which controlled the Oregon Territory, and with Mexico, which controlled most of the Southwest. Britain ceded the Oregon Territory to the United States in 1846, believing it not worth the struggle to maintain. However, Mexico and the United States fought two territorial wars, in 1830 and 1840, which resulted in the U.S. gaining Texas and much of California, New Mexico, and Arizona.

As the pioneers moved ever westward they came into conflict with the indigenous peoples. Frequently these confrontations were small frontier skirmishes, but sometimes United States' policy called for large-scale campaigns to remove or kill the Native Americans; indeed, by 1840 almost all of the Indians east of the Mississippi had been driven into Oklahoma. A tragic example of Indian removal is the Cherokee nation. The Cherokees held land in Alabama, North Carolina, Mississippi, and Georgia, and their nation had an emerging republican form of government. Many Cherokees were literate in their language, and, as a whole, they were becoming settled farmers like many southern whites. However, after fierce debate in Congress, they were forcibly moved to Oklahoma. Their journey is often called the Trail of Tears—a journey so harsh that one-quarter of the tribe perished along the way.

As the pioneers pushed beyond the Mississippi, the United States government continued to wage war on the Native Americans, who sometimes fought back. During the Great Sioux War of 1865–1867 and the Red River War of 1874–

1875, Native Americans attacked soldiers, prospectors, and others who threatened them. Finally subdued by the Army, they were gradually placed on reservations, generally in undesirable sections of the country. Some effort was made to teach them English and to assimilate them, at a cost to their own culture.

The settling of these new areas also posed issues regarding statehood: when and how should a territory become a state, and should the new state permit slavery? Congress established straightforward steps whereby a territory might become a state, but the sticky issue of slavery provoked heated debate. Many of the founding fathers recognized the immoral nature of this institution. (Washington had freed his slaves upon his death, and President Jefferson signed a bill that outlawed the slave trade beginning in 1808.) In the North, especially, there was strong antipathy to the institution; however, the South, with its vast fields of cotton, tobacco, and sugar, was dependent on slave labor. When Missouri applied for statehood in 1817, heated debate ensued about whether it should be admitted as a slave state; since it was the second state to be carved from the vast Louisiana Purchase, the decision would have ramifications for future states created from this territory. Until this moment, there had been parity between the admission into the Union of free and slave states, a practice that the South wanted to continue but the North did not. After intense argument, compromise was reached in 1820, when Missouri entered the Union as a slave state and Maine as a free state. Further, it was agreed that slavery would not be permitted in any state created from the Louisiana Purchase above the latitude of 36° 30′. The acrimony and fervor that this issue generated highlighted the great sectional differences between the North and South—differences that would erupt in the Civil War.

# The Union Tested: The Civil War and Reconstruction

The Civil War posed the greatest challenge to the United States in its history, generating enmity that persisted for generations, destroying the South's economy, and killing more Americans, over 618,000 of them, than any other American war. The institution of slavery—so essential to the South, anathema to the North—was the primary reason for this conflagration. Despite the Missouri Compromise of 1820, issues surrounding slavery continued to spawn tensions as more territories were added to the Union. Novels like *Uncle Tom's Cabin* (1852), which highlighted the abuses of slavery, and events like John Brown's raid on Harper's Ferry (1859), designed to incite a slave uprising, served to increase the rift. After several years of secessionist talk, South Carolina withdrew from the Union shortly after Abraham Lincoln's election as president of the United States. Eventually 10 additional Southern states followed suit, and, in early 1861, these states elected Jefferson Davis as president of their Confederacy. However, many citizens of the slaveholding "border states"—Kentucky, Missouri, Delaware, Maryland, and western Virginia (later to become West Virginia)—believed foremost in the Union, and Lincoln used a variety of measures to keep these states within the northern fold.

War broke out in April of 1861 when the South attacked Fort Sumter in Charleston, South Carolina, one of four federal forts not yet in Confederate hands. Which side would prevail in this war of brother against brother? The North certainly possessed many advantages. Its population was two-and-one-half times larger than the South's, it had far greater industrial capacity and wealth, and it contained almost three times more railroad track.[3] It also controlled the United States' navy, which blockaded the South throughout the war, albeit with limited success. And, of course, the North had Abraham Lincoln as its leader, one of the most intelligent, compassionate, and noble presidents in its history. Despite these advantages, the South possessed better military commanders for much of the war, as well as soldiers who fought with great zeal, eager to preserve their cherished way of life. The South also held the country's agrarian base and produced cotton, coveted not only by Northern manufacturers but also by the British and French. (For much of the war the North feared that these foreign powers might come to the aid of the South, driven by their thirst for cotton, although this never happened.) Finally, the South needed only to hold out, hoping that at some point the North would lose its appetite for war and would conclude it.

The war dragged on for four years, from 1861–1865. In the eastern United States, great Confederate generals like Robert E. Lee and Stonewall Jackson led their armies to multiple victories, especially during the early part of the war. Bloody battles such as Bull Run, Antietam, and Fredericksburg were fought at enormous cost to both sides; in the three-day Battle of Gettysburg, for example, the South suffered 28,000 casualties and the North, 23,000. In the Mississippi Valley, the Union general Ulysses S. Grant proved himself a determined and capable general; by the summer of 1863 his forces had gained control of the Mississippi River, thus bifurcating the South. In 1864 President Lincoln moved Grant to command the eastern army, which Grant did with success. By April

---

3.    Nevins and Commager, *A Pocket History*, 217.

1865 Grant's victories, coupled with other Union victories in the South, led Robert E. Lee to tender his sword at Appomattox. Tragically, President Lincoln was assassinated a few days after this, and Andrew Johnson, his vice president, assumed the presidency.

The 10-year period following the war, the Reconstruction period, was a difficult era in United States' history, and the status of the freed slaves was a major issue. President Lincoln had liberated the four million slaves in his Emancipation Proclamation of 1863 and had worked to pass the Thirteenth Amendment (January 1865), which prohibited slavery in the United States. At the war's conclusion, debate arose concerning the rights of the former slaves. Congress demanded that they receive full citizenship with equal rights, while President Johnson favored each state's right to determine their status. When some Southern states passed restrictive "black codes," Congress responded with the Fourteenth Amendment in June 1866, which granted citizenship to "all persons born or naturalized in the United States," and which made the federal government responsible for ensuring equal rights. Further, Congress mandated that Southern states would not be admitted into the Union unless they ratified this amendment. The Fifteenth Amendment, passed in 1869, clarified that no person could be denied suffrage because of his color or race. Great acrimony ensued between the executive and legislative branch during this time, and Congress impeached Johnson in 1868 for conspiring against the Constitution and Congress. Johnson narrowly escaped conviction. And, of course, it would take a century for the promise of "equal rights" to reach fruition in the South.

# Immigration

Throughout the 1800s—even during the Civil War—immigrants continued to enter the United States, making America a true melting pot, more so than many Americans desired by century's end. In the western United States, Chinese immigrants entered the country primarily through the port of San Francisco, creating a vast pool of cheap labor. These Chinese workers contributed significantly to the construction of the transcontinental railroad. In the northeastern United States, between 1840 and 1860, vast numbers of Irish, as well as many Germans, entered the country—4.2 million in all, a greater percentage relative to the native population than at any other period in history.[4] The Irish were the first wave of immi-

---

4.    Robert Divine et al., *America Past and Present*, Brief 3rd edition (New York: Harper Collins College Publishers, 1994), 211.

grants in the eastern U.S. who were significantly different from the newcomers of the past: they were Catholic rather than Protestant, and the majority was poor. Because they lacked the resources to buy land or travel far, they settled mostly in eastern urban areas. Eager for employment, they were willing to work long hours for low wages and thus displaced and antagonized many American-born laborers. Their vast numbers, however, helped accelerate America's industrial growth.

Beginning in 1870 a torrent of immigrants arrived who were also different from the mostly northern Europeans of earlier years. These were southern and eastern Europeans—Italians, Poles, Russians, and Austro-Hungarians—mostly Catholic or Jewish, frequently poor, sometimes illiterate, and, like the Irish, more apt to settle in cities than earlier immigrants. By 1890 over 15 percent of America's population was of foreign birth or parentage. In 1900, 80 percent of New York City's population was of foreign birth or parentage, and other major cities, such as Chicago and Boston, had a majority of foreign-born inhabitants.[5] As they flocked to the cities, the immigrants often formed their own churches and community organizations in an effort to preserve their heritage—and thus raised the question, would they ever truly become "American"? Their vast numbers tested the ability of schools to absorb them, of housing to accommodate them, and of public sanitation to deal with their refuse, and their willingness to work for low wages often pitted the American-born workers against them. By 1900 American sentiment demanded immigration quotas. Congress had restricted Chinese immigration in 1882, but an immigration law limiting Europeans and others did not take effect until 1917. New immigration laws continued to evolve throughout the 1900s as America sought to restrict entry into its land of promise.

## Industrialization: Magnates and Workers

During the 1800s the United States industrialized and its economy soared; its labor force and abundant resources fueled the process, and its burgeoning population provided ample markets for manufactured goods. Inventions such as electricity, the Corliss engine (a giant steam engine), and the construction of huge steel mills contributed to the new industrial age, while an explosion of railroad tracks, culminating in the completion of the transcontinental railroad in 1869, helped revolutionize the country's transportation system. Chain stores like A&P grocery or F.W. Woolworth spread across the country, while Sears, Roebuck targeted the rural consumer with its mail-order catalogues.

---

5.   Divine, *America Past and Present*, 323.

However, the United States also suffered from many of the problems that had confronted Europe during its industrialization: crowded and unsanitary housing, harsh working conditions, and exploitation of laborers. By the 1880s, "captains of industry" (or "robber barons" depending on one's perspective) such as Andrew Carnegie and John D. Rockefeller had reaped enormous wealth while workers often lived in squalid conditions and worked 10 hours a day, six days a week. The federal government, as well as state and local governments, supported the entrepreneurial spirit and was unwilling to impose economic regulations, which added to the divide between rich and poor. It would not be until President Franklin D. Roosevelt's New Deal legislation in the 1930s that the federal government actively sought to redress some of these socioeconomic inequities.

By the late 1800s, workers began to agitate for better working conditions and more pay. Indeed, 23,000 strikes, many of them bloody, occurred between 1880 and 1900, unsettling many Americans and making them question the benefits of industrialization.[6] Since government generally supported the bosses, rather than the striking laborers, little improvement occurred in working conditions. Labor unions such as the American Federation of Labor (AFL), which developed during the late 1800s, were committed to ameliorating the workers' plight, although they made little headway in the nineteenth century. However, beginning in the early twentieth century, states began passing laws to restrict child labor and to limit the hours that a woman could work. Although the federal government passed similar laws beginning in 1916, it would be the 1930s before real improvement was realized.

"City bosses," with their powerful political machines, did reach out to the immigrant-workers and others of the underprivileged. In New York City, for example, William "Boss" Tweed and his cronies located jobs for these people, provided them with food in times of need, contributed to hospitals and orphanages, and encouraged the immigrants towards citizenship. Highly corrupt, these city bosses nonetheless filled a need that the government failed to meet during this period. Journalists and clergy, too, called attention to the plight of the disadvantaged, which helped generate reform in some states.

## The Evolving Women's Movement

Elizabeth Cady Stanton and Lucretia Mott, among others, led a feminist movement agitating for women's suffrage. The work of these suffragettes culminated

---

6.   Ibid., 318.

in the Seneca Falls Convention of 1848, but failed to influence the federal government. However, in some western states women had received the right to vote in state elections: they had worked and suffered alongside their men as they sought to carve a life out of the wilderness, and had received the franchise in recognition of their contributions. These frontier people were also less bound by tradition than their brethren in the East, where women had not received the franchise in local or state elections. It would take a new century and a world war before all American women would attain the right to vote in state, as well as national, elections.

# 15

## *Intellectual Revolutions of the 1800s and Early 1900s*

The confluence of the dual revolutions, coupled with ideas of the Scientific Revolution and the Enlightenment, produced an intellectual revolution that began in the early 1800s and continued for a century. New ideologies emerged and older ideologies took new form. During this era intellectuals and scientists generated exciting and novel ideas that often shocked their contemporaries; these ideas took firm root and have greatly shaped the modern world.

## Liberalism: John Stuart Mill and Mary Wollstonecraft

Liberalism was one of the major ideas that influenced this era, evolving from the ideas of earlier thinkers like John Locke. Englishman John Stuart Mill (1806–1873) advocated political liberalism—the idea that a person should enjoy individual freedoms that were delineated in a constitution, freedoms that were the responsibility of the government to protect. Like Locke, he believed that the government should play a limited role in the lives of people, that people should be free to pursue their self-development without interference. Mill and other liberals folded into their ideas the Enlightenment belief in the inherent goodness and rationality of the individual; they held that free individuals would ensure societal progress. Mill also embraced the philosophy of utilitarianism, the idea that institutions and laws should work to promote the happiness of the people. To this end, he was an advocate for increased rights for women and workers, contending that both groups should have representation in Parliament. His ideas, and those of his cohorts, eventually led to universal suffrage in Britain and in other nations.

There were others who began agitating for women's rights during this period. In the late 1700s Mary Wollstonecraft (1759–1797), often deemed the first feminist, called for greater educational opportunities for women in order for them to become better wives and mothers. Throughout the 1800s the call for women's rights escalated, particularly within Britain and in the United States, as we saw in the last chapter. Feminists ultimately demanded the right to vote, and the suffragettes, as they were called, used militant tactics to achieve their goal. They participated in hunger strikes and demonstrations; one English suffragette even threw herself in front of a racehorse, perishing in the effort to bring attention to feminist demands. Women finally gained suffrage in many European nations and in America following the First World War.

The idea of liberalism also took hold in the economic sphere. Englishman Adam Smith, noted earlier (Chapter XIII), believed in a *laissez-faire* economy, one in which the government did not intervene in the workings of the marketplace. He promoted his ideas in *The Wealth of Nations* (1776), and is deemed the "father of capitalism." Another influential economic liberal was English clergyman Thomas Malthus (1766–1834), whose views were shaped by the burgeoning population resulting from the Industrial Revolution. He came to believe that famine, flood, pestilence, and war were nature's way of bringing excess population into correspondence with resources. He felt that government should not intervene to ameliorate suffering and death from these conditions; rather, it should allow the acts of nature to play out freely.

## Socialism and Communism

During this period the philosophy of socialism emerged in response to the abuses of the Industrial Revolution and to the idea of equality promoted by the French Revolution. One of the earliest socialists, Henri de Saint-Simon (1760–1825), believed that socialism was the logical extension of Christianity with its admonition to "love thy neighbor." Socialists believed that capitalism was morally wrong because it was ruthless: there were too many losers and not enough winners. They also believed that ownership should be collective rather than private—a factory, for example, should be owned by the government or by the workers. Finally, they held that a society's wealth should be distributed equally among its members. Karl Marx, whom we have noted earlier, was a socialist, but a revolutionary one, a communist. He agreed with socialism's tenets, but Marx called for an overthrow of capitalist society, and urged "Working men of all countries, unite!" Once the proletarian revolution had been accomplished, Marx envisioned a classless, stateless society—a utopia. The ideas of the socialists and communists found adherents in Europe and other parts of the globe and would greatly contribute to shaping the modern world.

## The Emergence of Nationalism

Perhaps the most powerful ideology spawned during this period was that of nationalism. Nationalism, literally "belief in one's nation," arose from a person's strong identification with others who shared a common history, the same language, and often the same religion and customs. The French Revolution had inspired great nationalism within France, especially when Napoleon and his army met with repeated victories. Moreover, as French armies swept across Europe, nationalism took firm root in other lands as subjugated peoples defined themselves as German or Spanish in opposition to the French. As we shall see, nationalism proved to be the driving force behind the unification of Germany and Italy in the nineteenth century. It also greatly contributed to the world wars of the twentieth century, and the breakup of empires and creation of new states following the wars. It continues to be a powerful force in today's world.

## The Giants: Darwin, Freud and Einstein

During this era the ideas of three men—Charles Darwin, Sigmund Freud, and Albert Einstein—had an immeasurable impact on the modern world. Their ideas amazed and startled their peers, and continue to generate admiration, and sometimes controversy, today.

Englishman Charles Darwin's (1809–1882) idea of evolution through natural selection was as revolutionary as Copernicus' heliocentric theory or Newton's laws of gravitation. Darwin came from a well-educated family of naturalists, and as a boy had heard his grandfather and others discuss the idea of evolution. However, though numerous scientists had considered the theory, Darwin was the first individual who would offer proof of it.

Darwin attended Cambridge University and upon graduation joined a scientific expedition aboard the *H.M.S. Beagle*, which traveled the globe from 1831–1836. As the naturalist aboard ship, Darwin collected and studied plants and animals throughout the voyage. It was in South America that Darwin discovered fossil remains of extinct animals that bore a similarity to modern species. On the Galapagos Islands Darwin noted variations among individual plants and animals of the same species. He argued that the variations—random gene changes, we now know—sometimes enabled certain individuals to adapt better for survival, thus allowing them to pass their particular adaptations to their descendents. Over time, Darwin argued, a whole new species might evolve through this natural selection, this "survival of the fittest." Darwin returned from his voyage, continued his studies, and in 1858 published his book *On the Origin of the Species by Means of Natural Selection.* His contention that evolutionary changes accounted for all species, even the human race, outraged and unsettled many Christians who believed in the divine creation of all living creatures. Darwin's theories, however, found increasing numbers of adherents over the decades.

Sigmund Freud (1856–1939), a Viennese physician, is often called "the father of psychoanalysis," and his groundbreaking ideas aroused, and continue to arouse, both adulation and scorn. Although others before him had studied human behavior, Freud's ideas were the most sweeping and influential. His revolutionary book *On Dreams,* published in 1900, developed the idea that the unconscious, which sometimes contains troubling memories stretching back to childhood, plays a major role in behavior. He believed that through dreams and free association, a trained therapist could access a patient's unconscious and thereby help to resolve behavioral issues. Freud also believed that two drives—sex and aggression—motivated most human action. He contended that starting from infancy, people pass through several psychological stages of sexual development; if they fail to pass successfully through one of these stages, they become fixated on an immature stage. Finally, Freud speculated that the human mind was divided in three parts: simply put, these parts are the id, our natural impulses; the superego, our conscience; and the ego, our sense of reality which mediates between the id and superego. He proposed that behavioral problems arose when either the id or superego was too strong.

Freud established the groundwork for modern psychology and psychiatry, and his ideas altered the way that people thought about human nature and behavior. His emphasis on the significance of childhood highlighted the importance of a nurturing environment for children, and his focus on human sexuality encouraged a healthy openness. His ideas also influenced the arts; one need only think of the stream-of-consciousness style of James Joyce's *Ulysses* or the exploration of the unconscious in Dali's surrealist paintings. Although Freud has his detractors, and although others have offered different explanations of human behavior, his ideas have most pervaded modern culture. Expressions like "Freudian slip," "Oedipus complex," "phallic symbol," and "transference" are part of common parlance.

Freud lived most of his life in Vienna, but, as a Jew, left Austria with his family shortly after the *Anschluss* (union) with Germany in 1938. He lived the last year of his life in England.

The German Albert Einstein (1879–1955) rivals Sir Isaac Newton as one of the greatest scientific minds in history. After graduating from university, Einstein worked in a Swiss patent office, which allowed him leisure time to work on his groundbreaking theories. In 1905, when just 26, he proposed his theory of relativity, the idea that the physical world is not an objective reality, but rather is relative to the eye of the beholder and is dependent on space, time and velocity. In the same year he published other papers, one that suggested the equivalence of mass and energy as expressed in the famous equation $E=mc^2$. This revolutionary idea, that energy might be released from the nucleus of atoms, eventually led to the creation of the atomic bomb and nuclear power. Additionally, Einstein put forth the notion that light consisted of tiny particles, called quanta, which led to the development of a branch of physics called quantum mechanics. His ideas explained the photoelectric effect, which helped to develop the photoelectric eye. During the later years of his life, Einstein worked on a unified field theory. He hoped to prove the feasibility of doing so, feeling that if he did not succeed, perhaps no one ever would.

His brilliant work led to university positions in Zurich, Prague and Berlin. In 1933, however, when Einstein was visiting the United States, the ascendant Nazi government seized his property and rescinded his citizenship, for Einstein was a Jew. Germany's loss was America's gain; Einstein joined the Institute for Advanced Studies at Princeton University and remained there for the rest of his life.

# The Arts in the Late 1800s and Early 1900s: The Beginning of Modernism

During the late 1800s, artists and intellectuals began to challenge the conventions of their day and to explore new possibilities in art, architecture, music, and literature. This break with tradition and emphasis on experimentation and innovation led to the movement called Modernism.

In this era artists began to move away from realistic renderings of their subjects—after all, the camera, invented in the mid 1800s, was able to perform this feat. The Impressionists—painters such as Frenchmen Claude Monet (1840–1926) and Auguste Renoir (1841–1919)—sought to capture the fleeting impression of a moment, exploring the play of light and dark on their subjects rather than recording the way that a haystack or a field of poppies really looked. Post-Impressionists like Vincent Van Gogh used intense color and charged lines to create deeply expressive works rather than perfectly representational ones. Paul Gauguin, another post-Impressionist, sought refuge from industrialized society in Tahiti, painting idyllic scenes of life there in an intentionally flat and primitive style. In the early 1900s the Spaniard Pablo Picasso (1881–1973) developed Cubism; his *Mademoiselles d'Avignon* (1907), perhaps the most revolutionary painting of the first half of the twentieth century, addressed the issue of how to render three-dimensional subjects on a two-dimensional surface. Thus his five "mademoiselles" are viewed from a multiplicity of perspectives, and their angled surfaces bear little resemblance to the true female form. Frenchman Henri Matisse (1869–1954), Picasso's contemporary, rivals him in influence. Matisse's interest was in color, not form, and his exuberant and brightly colored works underscore his statement that he wanted his art to be pleasurable to the viewer. Each of these painters focused on issues other than representing the objective world realistically; their works—experimental, unconventional, and challenging—baffled the public and often outraged the traditional art establishment.

There was also a fresh approach to architecture during this period. American Frank Lloyd Wright (1869–1959) was one of the leading iconoclasts, contending that it was not a building's exterior that was important, the conventional belief, but rather its interior rooms. He simplified the exteriors of his designs and focused on creating functional rooms that met the needs of the people using them. He frequently utilized construction materials from the surrounding area so that his buildings would blend into their environment.

Innovation occurred in music, too. Austrian Arnold Schoenberg (1874–1951) explored the possibilities of atonal music, using the 12 pitches of the octave as equals, often composing dissonant, nontraditional pieces. Russian Igor Stravinsky (1882–1971) also created unconventional works; his *Rite of Spring*, with its pulsating, disturbing sounds, caused Parisian theatergoers to riot in 1913 when they heard it and viewed the accompanying ballet.

Playwrights such as the Norwegian Henrik Ibsen (1828–1906) and Russian Anton Chekhov (1860–1904) also crafted works that challenged convention. Ibsen forthrightly addressed social issues of his day—the repression of women, the effects of venereal disease—and scandalized the public in doing so. His social realism would prove a major influence for subsequent writers. Chekhov explored the empty and feckless lives of his characters, their conversations often at cross-purposes; his works, too, would shape future playwrights.

As we shall see, it would take World War I, which smashed long-held beliefs and traditions, to create a climate in which the public would embrace these seminal works.

# 16

# *The Great War: World War I 1914–1918*

During the latter part of the nineteenth century, a confluence of events and ideas set the stage for World War I. The ambitions of Germany, a new European state, were a major cause of the war. The imperialistic scramble, which accelerated after 1880, was also significant because of the tensions generated when European nations competed for control of large sections of Africa and Asia. The notion that war was a glorious and heroic event took strong root during this period, leading to increased militarism: many European countries churned out weapons and developed their armies and navies. Indeed, as Stefan Zweig wrote in "The Rushing Feeling of Fraternity":

> What did the great mass know of war in 1914, after nearly half a century of peace? They did not know war, they had hardly given it a thought. It had become legendary, and distance had made it seem romantic and heroic.[1]

Finally, powerful feelings of nationalism among many European peoples contributed to the volatility of the period.

It is through hindsight that we can identify these factors as contributing to World War I. However, many Europeans and Americans of the late nineteenth and early twentieth centuries believed that they were living in the best of all possible worlds. This era has been called the *Belle Époque*, or beautiful age. Inventions such as electricity, the airplane, and the automobile, effective vaccines against some diseases, the evolution of the middle class, increased literacy, and 100 years of mostly peaceful European relations following the Napoleonic wars—all contributed to a sense of optimism and a belief in progress. Of course, the *Belle Époque* was a term coined, no doubt, by people of the upper classes. It

---

1.    Perry, Peden, von Laue, *Sources*, II: 303.

was not a beautiful age for the majority of people, who still lived by the sweat of their brow.

# Preface to the War: Germany and Italy Become Nation States

Unlike the citizens of England, France, and Spain, the German people of the Holy Roman Empire and the inhabitants of the Italian peninsula had not coalesced into their own nation states. As we have noted earlier, the Holy Roman Empire consisted of a loose confederation of princes and their principalities, headed by an emperor, who, in truth, held little sway over the princes and their kingdoms. The Italian peninsula, meanwhile, had just one independent area governed by Italians, the kingdom of Piedmont-Sardinia. Austria dominated much of the north and a branch of the Bourbons, a French and Spanish ruling family, controlled the south. The Roman Catholic Church administered the Papal States, which stretched across central Italy.

The German states united in 1871 under the leadership of Otto von Bismarck (1815–1898), prime minister and foreign minister of Prussia. Prussia was one of the most influential German states and had a strong militaristic background. Bismarck used "blood and iron," that is, a series of small wars, to bring about unification, realizing that nothing brings a people together more effectively than fighting against a common enemy. The final piece of his strategy involved a short-lived, six-month war with France, the Franco-Prussian war of 1870–1871, in which all the German principalities, still smarting from the wars of Louis XIV and Napoleon, united against France. As the war drew to a close, the German princes proclaimed Wilhelm I, the former Holy Roman Emperor, as the Kaiser of the new Germany. In 1888 Wilhelm II succeeded his father, with dire consequences.

Wilhelm II had great aspirations for his new nation: he wanted Germany to have its "place in the sun" and articulated his policy for the nation as one of *Weltpolitik*, world politics. In order for Germany to become a major player on the world stage, Wilhelm developed a large German army and navy and seized colonies in Africa and Asia for his fledgling nation. Contributing to Wilhelm's ability to develop his army and navy was the fact that by 1900 Germany was highly industrialized, second in the world to Britain.

A year earlier, in 1870, Italy had united and become a nation. For decades there had been calls for Italian unification; Guiseppe Mazzini (1805–1872), the "heart" of the *Risorgimento (*unification movement), had sought to inspire Italians to drive out the Bourbons and Austrians. This was largely accomplished under the leadership of Count Camilo di Cavour (1810–1861), the foreign minister of Piedmont-Sardinia; an astute and pragmatic politician, he has been dubbed the "head" of the unification movement. He made Piedmont-Sardinia a model state for the rest of Italy to emulate and he negotiated treaties that helped lead to unification. Guissepe Garibaldi (1807–1882), "the sword" behind Italian nationhood, led his band of Red Shirts from Sicily northwards to help unify the peninsula. Italy became a constitutional monarchy with Victor Emanuel, the King of Piedmont-Sardinia, as the first King of Italy. Italians would ultimately want to demonstrate to the world that they, too, were a nation to be reckoned with—but this would happen after World War I under Mussolini.

# The Underlying Causes of World War I

# The Age of Imperialism

Beginning in the late 1800s, European nations, and the United States and Japan to a lesser degree, began dividing up the less-developed parts of the globe in what has been called an imperialistic "scramble." Rabid nationalism was the overarching reason for their behavior, but more specific reasons may be factored in. Certainly, economic motives were a driving force: these industrialized nations needed raw materials to fuel their burgeoning economies, and they needed overseas markets in which to sell their manufactured goods. The resources and peoples of Africa and Asia met these needs. The notion of the "white man's burden," as Rudyard Kipling expressed it, also contributed to the scramble. This was the idea that the civilized white races had a duty to the "heathens" to educate and to protect them; missionaries and others sought to save these peoples from everlasting perdition by spreading the Christian faith and by establishing schools and medical clinics. The concept of "social Darwinism" was invoked to justify these actions—for, the argument went, just as there were "fitter" species in the animal kingdom, there were also higher races among the human species. The greater economic and military power of the white races proved that they were superior to the colored races and deserved, therefore, to rule them. Finally, there was the sense that a powerful nation deserved an overseas empire as a symbol of its greatness; the people and the press of countries often pressured their governments into taking aggressive actions.

As you might imagine, the competition for territory generated tensions. Although the astute Otto von Bismarck organized a conference in Berlin in 1884 to discuss rules for the land grab, there were, nonetheless, hard feelings generated by the imperialistic race.

## The Glorification of War

Perhaps because a European-wide war hadn't been fought for almost a century, new generations forgot the scourge of war. Heinrich von Treitschke, an influential German historian writing in the late 1800s, propounded the notion that "war brings progress and becoming."[2] His ideas were widely, and tragically, embraced. This idealization of war contributed to increased militarism in Europe, and industrialization allowed many European nations to mass-produce weapons at unprecedented rates.

## Nationalism and International Relations

As nations committed to building ever-larger armies and navies and to stockpiling more weapons, there emerged a certain psychological preparedness for war. When Kaiser Wilhelm II, for example, in pursuit of German greatness, began building up his navy (in his view he had a right to any size navy that he wanted) the British became apprehensive. For centuries they had relied on their navy to protect their island home, and they viewed another large and modern European navy as a threat. The French looked with distress at Germany's growing army; in their view, they needed an even larger army to deter the Germans from aggressive behavior. Additionally, the French greatly resented the fact that the Germans had taken Alsace-Lorraine from them as part of the war booty following the Franco-Prussian war. As a matter of pride, they wanted this territory back. So beginning in the 1890s, the British and French had a natural affinity for each other, against what they perceived to be an aggressive, belligerent Germany.

Germany was not without friends, however. Its neighbor, Austria-Hungary, a large, polyglot empire, and one that was not very industrialized, was headed up by a German-speaking Habsburg emperor, Franz Joseph. Austria-Hungary was pleased that its cousin Germany was a strong nation and could be relied upon for support. One of Franz Joseph's major challenges was keeping his empire together. The Slavs, Czechs, Slovaks, Hungarians, and other peoples that consti-

---

2.    Ibid., 294.

tuted his empire were restive, and many of them wanted to form their own country. Especially irksome to maintaining the coherence of his empire were the neighboring Slavs of the Balkans, who wanted to form their own pan-Slavic nation, and who actively encouraged the Slavs of Austria-Hungary to throw off the shackles of the Habsburgs and to unite with them. Italy, too, looked to Germany as a friend. Italy was determined to have some land in North Africa and feared that France had designs on its interests there. So, by 1914, Germany, Austria-Hungary and Italy had established an alliance.

Tsar Nicholas II of Russia had his own aspirations—more sway over the Balkan area, for one. Russia hoped that if it aided the formation of a pan-Slavic nation, a "Yugoslavia," it would have influence in the region. Since Russia itself contained many Slavs, supporting its brothers in the Balkans seemed a natural choice. However, because Russia supported the Slavs in their ambitions, this put it in direct opposition to Austria-Hungary, and indirectly at odds with Austria-Hungary's ally, Germany.

We should note that Russia also had some domestic problems. The liberal reforms that had come to much of Europe during the past two centuries had not arrived in Russia; since the early 1800s a variety of revolutionary groups, often comprised of the intelligentsia (well-educated Russians), had dedicated themselves to overthrowing the repressive tsars and introducing liberal changes. Additionally, Russia had begun to industrialize in the late 1890s, and workers in cities like St. Petersburg were suffering the hardships and abuses that sprang from industrialization, just as their Western European brethren had generations before. These disgruntled urban workers represented a potential revolutionary force. Furthermore, Russian peasants, 80 percent of the population, were more impoverished and less educated than the peasants of Western Europe; they, too, represented a possible incendiary element.

Finally, we should make brief note of the Ottoman Empire, the remnants of the great Muslim Empire that had supplanted the Byzantine Empire. This empire had been shrinking since the early 1800s as nationalistic groups in places like Greece and the Balkans fought for independence. It was largely unindustrialized, and therefore weak relative to most European nations; its control of the Bosporus and Dardanelles gave it some strategic power, however. Russia, especially, looked longingly at control of these straits, which would provide it access to the Mediterranean. Recognizing Russia's desire for control of some of its territory led the Ottoman Empire to become an ally of Germany and Austria-Hungary.

Although some of these countries had shifting alliances with each other, by 1914 Germany, Italy and Austria-Hungary were members of a Triple Alliance; in looser alliance were Britain, France and Russia. These alliances, coupled with the factors enumerated above, created a situation ripe for explosion. The moment came in July 1914, when Gavrilo Princip, member of a Serbian nationalist terrorist group, assassinated Archduke Franz Ferdinand of Austria-Hungary.

## World War I: The Major Engagements

World War I has a special heartbreak about it. A generation of young men set off for war, buoyed by the notion that it was "sweet and proper" (*Dulce et Decorum Est* in the words of English poet Wilfred Owen) to die for one's country. Their romanticism was soon lost in the horrors of trench warfare that led to carnage on a scale rarely witnessed before in history. New types of weapons—efficient machine guns, poison gas, submarines, and long-range shells—coupled with old military strategy, contributed to an enormous casualty rate.

After the assassination of the Austrian archduke, the alliance system came into play and during August 1914, most of Europe became engulfed in war. Germany, Austria-Hungary, the Ottoman Empire, and later Bulgaria, allied as the Central Powers; Britain, France and Russia fought together and were called the Allies. Italy remained neutral for the first part of the war, feeling that Germany and Austria-Hungary were aggressors and that by the terms of their alliance, it did not have to support them. After promises of land from the Allies, Italy joined the war on their side in 1915.

In the first days of the war, the Germans marched through neutral Belgium (an outrage that brought Britain into the war) and sought to encircle Paris in a pincer-type movement. If Paris fell, the Germans reasoned that all of France would succumb. The French rallied, however: taxicabs from Paris were enlisted to speed troops to the front and the Germans were pushed back to the River Marne. The first major battle of the war, the Battle of the Marne, lasted five days and was emblematic of all that would unfold over the next four and a half years on the Western Front. During this first great battle, from September 6th to September 12th, there were roughly 1.6 million casualties—a huge number of dead and wounded that presaged the future slaughter. Following this battle, the Germans and French both dug in, and by December of 1914 a system of trenches stretched 375 miles from the English Channel to the Swiss border. In some places the enemy trenches were but a few hundred yards apart, in other places a mile or two. Barbed wire placed in "no man's land" between the trenches offered illusory protection. As positions became fixed in the trenches, a stalemate developed on the Western Front.

This system of trenches became the defining factor of the war on the Western Front. As the war evolved, each side constructed a series of interconnecting trenches stretching back from the front lines. Soldiers often built bunkers into the sides of trenches, some of which, especially on the German side, had electricity and other comforts of home. However, the overriding experience of trench life was one of misery. The trenches often filled with water and men's feet became swollen with the continual damp, a condition known as trench foot. The filth and the body lice, the presence of rats that grew especially fat feasting on corpses, days and nights of constant shelling, and long stretches of inactivity and boredom, all contributed to the soldiers' sense that they were, indeed, in hell.

The most dreaded moment of trench life was the general's command to go "over the top," through no-man's land and into the enemy's trenches—offensive action designed to break the stalemate. A general's ambition was rarely realized, however: the soldiers were clear targets as they emerged, and the enemy's rapid-fire machine guns mowed down thousands. Indeed, the machine gun has often been called the premier weapon of WWI because it proved so lethal in trench warfare.

On the Eastern Front, after an initial Russian incursion into Germany, the Germans defeated the Russians time and again. During those instances in which the Austro-Hungarians and the Ottomans seemed to be flagging in their efforts against the Russians, the Germans sent support. The Russian losses should by no means reflect on their army's valor, however, for the soldiers were mostly poorly equipped and badly trained peasants. Historians estimate, for example, that one in three Russian soldiers was without a rifle as he went into combat; each man was therefore ordered to pick up a fallen comrade's weapon to secure one for himself.

There is a certain method to the madness of WWI, as countries sought to utilize strategies that would achieve victory. In 1915 Winston Churchill, head of the British Admiralty, decided to bring the war to the East, to the realm of the Ottomans, since a deadlock prevailed in the trenches of Western Europe. Churchill's plan aimed to use the British navy, some of its army, and a host of troops from its Empire (Australians, New Zealanders, and Indians, for example) to attack the Ottoman Turks along the Dardanelles at a site called Gallipoli. Once the Allied forces had secured the Dardanelles, they would move on to Constantinople; with this city under Allied control, the Ottomans would surely lose heart and surrender. Additionally, Churchill wanted to get supplies to Britain's suffering ally,

Russia. Alas, Churchill's plan failed; for months the Ottomans, reinforced by the Germans, shelled and shot at the Allied forces, such that after ten months the Allies withdrew. The cost to the Allies and to the Turks was enormous. In fact, so many Australians perished in this battle that the Aussies pledged never again to fight in a European war that had no direct impact on them; they date their independence from Britain to the battle of Gallipoli.

In 1915 the British and the German navies engaged in the one major sea battle of World War I, the Battle of Jutland off the coast of Denmark. Neither nation wanted to risk its navy in direct combat—a good example of the deterrence theory in warfare—and the navies met by chance. In the ensuing combat the British suffered more casualties and a greater loss of their ships, but since the German fleet never again ventured into the North Sea, most historians regard the Battle of Jutland as a British victory.

By 1916 frustration was mounting among the generals: they wanted to take some definitive action to break the stalemate on the Western Front, in particular. In February of that year, the Germans initiated a major assault on Verdun in eastern France, hoping to "bleed the French to death." In fact, there were almost as many German casualties (330,000) during the 11 months of battle as there were French (350,000). In the first day of battle, the Germans launched one million shells into the area of Verdun! It is easy to see how the term "shell-shocked" arose.

As pressure mounted on the French at Verdun—over 70 percent of its army would rotate through the hell there—they called upon their British allies to mount an offensive to relieve them. This the British did at the Battle of the Somme in northeastern France in early July 1916. During the first day of battle 60,000 British soldiers died or were wounded as they went "over the top" and were mowed down by the Germans, the single worst day in British military history. The Battle of the Somme slogged on for months, finally ending in November. Only a bit of land had been won at a cost of 400,00 British, 200,000 French, and 500,00 German casualties.

# Two Major Changes in 1917:

# Revolution in Russia

Two events occurred in 1917 that had major effects on the war: the Russian Revolution, which led to Russia's withdrawal from WWI, and the entrance of the United States into the war.

Underlying problems contributed to the toppling of Tsar Nicholas II and his government, many of which were exacerbated by the war. First, the institution of the tsar was a repressive and antiquated one; most tsars possessed little sense of obligation to the people of Russia, or had much concern for promoting the common good. They had traditionally relied on strict censorship, secret police and harsh labor camps to maintain their control. This put the institution of the tsar in striking contrast to the constitutional monarchies of Western Europe; many educated Russians, as well as others, chafed at this situation and fervently desired change. Moreover, Tsar Nicholas II, a handsome, loving husband and father, was a weak personality, committed to ruling as an autocrat but without the attributes necessary to do so effectively. In 1915 he made the ill-fated decision to go to the Russian front to lead his troops in battle. As losses mounted and supplies grew short, Russians came to perceive World War I as "the tsar's war," adding to his unpopularity.

Additionally, the tsar had left his wife Alexandra at home to run the government; she was under the sway of Rasputin, a self-proclaimed priest to whom both she and Nicholas had turned when he had seemingly ameliorated their son's hemophilia. The influence of Rasputin undermined support for the tsar by those groups that had traditionally backed him, the nobles and the Russian Orthodox Church.

Another factor contributing to the revolution was the disgruntled factory workers in St. Petersburg. Suffering from inadequate housing, long work hours, and unsafe factory conditions, they were now faced with food shortages; the peasants were off fighting and the crop yields were low. As we know, nothing fuels anger like an empty belly.

Finally, revolutionary groups had long been committed to promoting change within Russia, and they were now busy at the war front, stirring up the soldiers and undermining their already wavering commitment to the war. The soldiers, most of them peasants, yearned to go home to work their fields, to support their wives, children, and other relations.

All these factors coalesced in March 1917 when the hungry and dispirited workers of St. Petersburg went on strike. When the soldiers refused to fire on them, the tsar abdicated and a temporary government was formed, devoted to the liberal principals that guided Western European governments. However, this Provisional government's commitment to remaining in WWI ultimately led to its downfall: Russians wanted out of the war. Another political group, the Bolsheviks, pledged to leave the war; its slogan "Peace, Land and Bread" resonated with many Russians, and Vladimir Lenin and Leon Trotsky led the Bolsheviks to power in late 1917. Lenin carried through on the promise of peace, and in March 1918 Russia signed the Treaty of Brest-Litovsk with Germany. Sometimes dubbed the "rape of Russia" because of its harsh terms, the treaty highlights Lenin's eagerness to end involvement in the war in order to focus on building communism in Russia. As you might imagine, the Germans were gleeful at Russia's withdrawal from the war: now they had just one front with which to concern themselves.

Nonetheless, there were Russians who did not want their country governed by Lenin and his cronies, and a three-year civil war ensued in which millions perished. During this same period, Lenin was busy imposing state control over the economy and over many aspects of Russian life, creating the world's first communist state.

## The United States Enters the War

America joined the war in 1917; its historic ties to Britain and to France, the German violation of neutral Belgium at the war's beginning, the German sinking of the passenger ship *Lusitania* in 1915 which resulted in over one hundred American deaths—all contributed to the U.S. favoring the Allies. Then, in 1917, the Germans sent a telegram to Mexico, the Zimmerman note, which promised Mexico land in the United States if it would join the German war effort against the United States. The telegram, intercepted by the British, outraged the Americans when they learned of its contents and propelled them into a declaration of war. By 1918 the Americans had landed on French soil in full force and these ebullient, well-fed troops turned the tide of the war. In battles such as Chateau-Thierry and the Argonne Forest the combined Allied forces defeated the worn-out and ill-supplied German troops. An armistice was called and a peace treaty signed on the 11$^{th}$ hour of the 11$^{th}$ day of the 11$^{th}$ month of 1918. For years following the war, Veterans' Day in the U.S., November 11$^{th}$, was called Armistice Day in commemoration of the conclusion of World War I.

## The Results of the Great War

Ten million dead, 20 million wounded—the flower of a generation was lost in the carnage of the Great War. It has been estimated that one Frenchmen died for every minute of the war, and even more Germans and Russians perished. The eastern French countryside was devastated; even today, in WWI battle sites, visitors are admonished to keep to the path since unexploded shells still present a danger. Moreover, people were disillusioned, cynical, alienated; gone was the pre-war optimism and idealism, lost in the horror of the trenches.

In January 1919, negotiators from more than 30 nations descended on Paris to discuss the terms of the war's settlement, although the "big three" leaders had the most influence during the conference. One of the major players was President Woodrow Wilson of the United States; often called "the Idealist," his major goals were to "make the world safe for democracy," to establish new countries based on the principle of national self-determination, and to create a League of Nations that would, through discussion and arbitration, obviate further wars. Another key figure, David Lloyd-George, prime minister of Britain, has often been dubbed "the Mediator." He wanted to punish Germany for its role in the war, but he also recognized that an economically strong Germany was essential for the resurrection of the European economy. Additionally, he feared the new communist country, the Soviet Union, and felt that a strong Germany in central Europe would help prevent the potential spread of communism across the continent. The third influential negotiator, Premier Georges Clemenceau of France, called "the Tiger," wanted outright revenge on Germany. Germany had started the war and it deserved punishment! It is worth noting that Germany had a delegation at the Paris Peace Conference, but members of its delegation served only as observers: Germany had no representation, no voice. Although Wilson got his League of Nations, and although 10 new countries[3] were created, on the whole, Clemenceau had his way: Germany was punished, and punished severely. Some terms of the treaty that angered Germans (and which Adolf Hitler would invoke years later) were as follows: Germany was to return Alsace-Lorraine to France; its army and navy were vastly reduced; Germany was forbidden to have an air force or U-boat fleet; it was to admit responsibility for starting WWI; and it had to pay war reparations, which were set at $33 billion, an enormous sum. Additionally, the border region between France and Germany, the heavily industrialized German Rhineland, would become a demilitarized zone, thereby offering some peace of mind to the French who demanded a buffer state between themselves and Germany. Ultimately, the new German government, the Weimar government, signed the unpopular Treaty of Versailles. In evaluating the treaty, Marshall Foch, the French commander of the Allied forces, perspicaciously stated that it was "an armistice that would last 20 years."

---

3.    Estonia, Latvia, Lithuania, Finland, Turkey, Yugoslavia, Czechoslovakia, Austria, Hungary and Poland

However, despite the many terrible effects of the war, it must be said that there is some merit to Treitschke's idea that "war brings progress," for WWI did have some positive results. In many European nations a loosening of class barriers occurred; rich and poor had worked side-by-side during the long years of war, and this had served to weaken class lines. Moreover, death—which had felled people from all classes—was also a great equalizer. Labor unions gained greater credibility with the public in light of their mighty efforts during the war. Women in many countries, including Britain and the United States, attained the vote in recognition of their contributions throughout the war. Advances took place in medicine and surgery, and the beginnings of plastic surgery evolved during this period. Finally, the mass production of automobiles and other goods became highly efficient, and commercial aviation and radio stations emerged after the war.

The League of Nations, on which President Wilson had pinned his hopes for the future, suffered from several problems. From the outset it was plagued by a lack of key members: the United States never joined the League, and Germany and the Soviet Union participated only briefly. Britain and France emerged as the power brokers, making the League very Eurocentric. Although this body did take some positive actions in the 1920s, settling a few border issues, working to outlaw slavery, and helping to improve global working conditions, it lacked the power to resolve most international disputes or to prevent acts of aggression.

## The Impact of World War I on Culture

Although artists like Pablo Picasso and Henri Matisse, as well as composers like Igor Stravinsky, had introduced challenging works before the war, the public accepted their revolutionary pieces with more alacrity following the war. After all, in a world where commonly held ideals and traditions had been smashed, new and often disturbing works seemed to express the alienation of the age. Poets like T.S. Eliot (1888–1965) in *The Wasteland* and William Butler Yeats (1865–1939) in *The Second Coming*, captured the pessimism of the period through verse. Artists such as German painters Max Beckmann (1884–1950) and George Grosz (1893–1959), and Italian sculptor Alberto Giacometti (1901–1966), illustrated the sense of "things falling apart" and of isolation, while Surrealist artist Salvador Dali (1904–1989) painted inscrutable and unsettling dream-like images. Writers James Joyce (1882–1941) and Virginia Woolf (1882–1941), liberated from traditional literary forms by the war, used an innovative stream-of-consciousness technique in their novels.

Across the ocean in the U.S., the Harlem Renaissance emerged, a celebration of black Americans' heritage and culture. This movement resulted from the Great Migration of rural southern blacks to northern cities in quest of employment before and during the war. As they came together in large numbers in cities like Chicago and New York, these African-Americans had the opportunity to interact with each other and to forge an identity more readily than they had in the rural South. Additionally, the black soldiers who fought in the Great War did so with great valor; their actions engendered enormous pride in African-Americans, which also contributed to the flowering of the Harlem Renaissance. During the 1920s and 1930s, black artists, writers, and musicians explored their roots and celebrated their peoples' contributions to American culture.

# 17

# *The Period between the Wars;*
# *World War II Begins*
# *1919–1939*

World War I had been fought in Europe with devastating effect on populations, farmland, and industry. In global terms, Europe was no longer the dominant player in the world—the U.S. and Japan were contenders for that role—nor was it the most affluent region of the globe as it had been. In fact, after the Great War most European nations were debtor nations, while the U.S. and Japan emerged as creditor nations. Additionally, after the war many European nations embraced democracy for the first time. Would it take hold and flourish, or would the trials of the postwar period undermine the democratic process in these fledgling states? This question was answered in Italy when Benito Mussolini ascended to power in 1922.

## The 1920s: Italy, Germany, the U.S.S.R., and the United States

## Italy

Mussolini, born in 1875, may best be described as an opportunist and bully, a lethal one upon occasion. After his military service in WWI, he engaged in socialist activities; when the socialist message found little appeal in postwar Italy, he switched political positions and promoted fascism, an ideology that rejected democracy, socialism, and communism. Rather, fascism promoted the idea of the State as an absolute, "in comparison with which individuals or groups are relative, only to be conceived of in their relation to the State."[1] Mussolini reminded

---

1.    Perry, Peden and von Laue, *Sources,* II: 365.

the Italians of their noble heritage—the great Roman Empire—and promised them that they would rise again. Mussolini stressed action over thought, glorified war, and embraced imperialism. He averred, "… the growth of empire … is an essential manifestation of vitality."[2] His ideas resonated with many Italians, and he would begin to fulfill his imperialistic ambitions in the early 1930s.

Mussolini gained power by forming his own army, the Black Shirts, which fought street battles with Communists and Socialists and administered large doses of castor oil to political opponents. He threatened, and then carried out, a march on Rome with his army to seize power in 1922. Succumbing to this threat, the Italian emperor Victor Emmanuel obligingly made Mussolini the head of state, as was the emperor's right under the Italian constitution. Mussolini thus came to power through legal means, but as a result of aggressive activities.

Once in power Mussolini slowly rescinded the rights of the Italian people and consolidated his power. He was called *Il Duce*, the leader, and as leader he delivered rousing speeches, undertook massive construction projects and created the sense that his was a modern and efficient state. So impressive was he that admirers flocked to Italy to witness his achievements; one of these, Adolf Hitler, would take fascism to a new level in the following decade. Although Mussolini was a dictator, he never was as ruthless and controlling as his fellow dictators, Hitler and Stalin. Indeed, between 1926 and 1944 he sentenced 23 political prisoners to death;[3] contrast this to the millions that perished under Hitler and Stalin.

# Germany

In Germany, the newly established democratic Weimar Republic had to contend with many issues. First, this government was tainted in the eyes of many Germans because it had signed the unpopular Treaty of Versailles. Additionally, the concept of democracy was relatively new to the German peoples and unsettling to some: they had been accustomed to one leader, an emperor, directing their country. The Weimar government also had to deal with hyperinflation that plagued Germany during the early 1920s, and which effectively wiped out the middle classes. So terrible was this inflation that, for example, people had to cart wheelbarrows of money to a bakery to purchase one loaf of bread. When Germany was unable to make its reparation payments in 1923, France and Belgium invaded the

---

2.   Ibid.
3.   John P. McKay, et al., *A History of Western Society*, vol. II (Boston: Houghton Mifflin Company, 1995), 981.

Rhineland and demanded payment in kind from the coalmines of the region. (And remember, the Rhineland was a demilitarized zone, and its invasion was a violation of international law.) The political and economic situation was indeed desperate.

However, to ameliorate the situation in Germany and in Europe more generally, the U.S. introduced the Dawes Plan in 1924. The brainchild of American banker and senator Charles Dawes, the plan called for the U.S. and some European nations to make loans to Germany so that it could regain economic stability. Once this was accomplished, Germany would repay its war debts to European nations so that they could ultimately satisfy their loans with the U.S. This plan was highly effective, and by the end of the decade the German economy was flourishing (although only Finland paid off its entire war debt to America). The Locarno Pacts of 1925 also brought peace of mind to Germany, as well as to other European nations. Under the terms of these agreements, Britain and Italy promised to come to the assistance of whichever country—Germany, France, Belgium—was threatened by the other. Finally, in 1928 many countries of the world signed the Kellogg-Briand Pact that outlawed war as a means of settling disputes. These actions contributed to a time of economic and political stability, an "era of fulfillment," as it is called, within Germany and in Europe at large.

# The U.S.S.R

In Russia, renamed the Union of Soviet Socialist Republics (also called the Soviet Union), Lenin and his followers had fought a savage internecine war before gaining control of the country. Even as civil war was waged, Lenin sought to transform Russia into a true communist nation. All businesses came under the sway of the state. Food battalions took food from the peasants and delivered it to the city dwellers following the Marxist dictum "from each according to his abilities to each according to his needs." However, the fighting and swift economic changes had a devastating effect on the U.S.S.R. and, under his New Economic Policy, Lenin rescinded some of his dramatic communist actions and restored some private ownership to smaller enterprises. Lenin died in 1924, and after a power struggle between Joseph Stalin and Leon Trotsky, Stalin emerged as the new leader of the Soviet Union in 1927.

Stalin was paranoid, cruel, and ruthless, a dictator who molded Russia into a totalitarian society. He allowed no challenges, real or perceived, to himself or to the Communist party. His KGB, the secret police, rounded up millions of suspects during his rule, and most of these suspects, if not killed outright, were sent to the *gulag*, the system of labor camps throughout the U.S.S.R. Being sent to the *gulag* was, in essence, a death sentence since most inmates died during their first year of incarceration. Stalin also used propaganda and mass rallies to glorify himself and the state, exercised strict censorship over the media, and abrogated other personal freedoms. Additionally, he closed most churches (remember, in Marxist teaching religion is the "opiate of the masses") and offered up, instead, a "cult of Stalin." Finally, he instituted a command economy in which the state took control of all aspects of the economy.

Indeed, when Stalin assumed power he immediately established ambitious economic goals for his country. He felt that the U.S.S.R. must "modernize or perish" and to this end he promoted the growth of heavy industry—oil, steel, electricity—at the expense of consumer goods. He established new industrial cities in eastern Russia and forcibly moved people there. He also had goals for the peasants—they must produce more grain and raise more livestock—and the government exacted heavy taxes on them, seizing grain and livestock for the cities. Eventually, Stalin collectivized the peasants, organizing them into large communal farms, believing that this would ensure more efficiency in agricultural output. The peasants initially resisted these measures, but when Stalin ruthlessly "liquidated" resisters, they were forced to comply. By the late 1930s, Stalin had realized his ambitions: the Soviet Union was approximating his industrial and agricultural goals.

In generalizing about the rest of Europe, suffice it to say that after a difficult period following World War I, most countries experienced some economic recovery. Britain and France, by the late 1920s, had regained their economic vigor, and democracy was taking root in new countries such as Czechoslovakia and Austria.

# The United States

Across the Atlantic in the United States, the "roaring Twenties" was underway. Women gained the vote, and with it a growing sense of independence as they bobbed their hair, shortened their skirts, and dared to smoke in public. The Harlem Renaissance (Chapter XVI), a movement encouraging and celebrating the talents of African-Americans, emerged in New York City. The NAACP (National Association for the Advancement of Colored People) formed during this time, and men like W.E.B. Dubois began calling for more rights for blacks. Economically, America recovered quickly from the expense of war; mass production, greatly improved during the war, ensured a steady stream of consumer goods. Politically, the United States increasingly retreated from the international scene. Reflecting this isolationist stance, the U.S. Senate, for a host of reasons, failed to ratify U.S. participation in the League of Nations, and the U.S. never joined this world organization.

## The Stock Market Crash and Great Depression

However, on October 24, 1929, "Black Tuesday," the U.S. stock market collapsed with profound consequences—and with even greater effects on Europe a year or so later. There were several reasons for the collapse. During the 1920s wages failed to keep pace with the cost of living, but, meanwhile, industry kept producing more and more goods, more than consumers needed or could afford. When their products failed to sell, factory owners had to release some workers, which meant that even more people would not have the means to purchase goods. In a vicious downward cycle, more workers were laid off and more products failed to sell. Compounding this trend was the fact that many people had bought into the stock market on "margin." By placing just 10 percent down on a stock—and borrowing the rest from a broker—people could own a particular stock with the expectation that they could sell it quickly at a higher price. They would then be able to pay the broker what they owed and still reap a profit. Alas, individuals began selling their stocks when it became apparent that an economic slowdown was at hand. Panic overwhelmed stockholders in late October 1929, and the market "crashed," ushering in the Great Depression.

## The 1930s: Hitler, Mussolini, Stalin, and the Start of WWII

The Depression took hold in Europe in the early 1930s, with dire consequences for Germany. The German Nazi Party promised a solution for Germany's economic woes, and many Germans were swayed by the rhetoric of Adolf Hitler, the Nazi party's most impassioned speaker.

Born in Austria in 1889, Hitler had, by all accounts, a lonely childhood. Orphaned by 19, he moved to Vienna hoping to gain entrance to the Imperial Academy of Fine Arts, which he failed to do. He remained in Vienna for several years, leading an impoverished and mostly friendless existence. It was World War I that saved Hitler. Wounded four times in his capacity as a messenger, he emerged from this war with a clear vision of the German peoples' greatness and with a desire to overturn the humiliating Treaty of Versailles. He joined the Nazi party following the war and was imprisoned for about a year after attempting a *putsch*, a seizure of the German government, in 1923. During his imprisonment he wrote his infamous *Mein Kampf—My Struggle*—which clearly spelled out his twisted ideology and many of his future goals. He celebrated the Aryan race: "If we divide humanity into three categories: into founders of culture, bearers of culture, and destroyers of culture, the Aryan would undoubtedly rate first. He established the foundation and walls of all human progress."[4] He repeatedly voiced his rabid anti-Semitism: "The Jew offers the most powerful contrast to the Aryan … the Jew is the big rabble-rouser for the destruction of Germany…. If our people and our state become the victims of blood-thirsty and money-thirsty Jewish tyrants, the whole world will be enmeshed in the tentacles of this octopus."[5] And he also spoke of the necessity for more *Lebensraum*, or living space, for Germany. In a statement that Stalin might have noted, Hitler concluded: "If we speak today about gaining territory in Europe, we think primarily of Russia and its border states."[6]

During the "era of fulfillment," the period of economic stability from the mid-to-late 1920s, the Nazi message had little appeal for Germans. However, beginning in the early 1930s when the Great Depression took hold, the Nazi party found more adherents, and in the 1932 Reichstag elections (the lower house of the German parliament) the Nazis won 37 percent of the vote, becoming the largest party. In January 1933, the president of Germany, the aged WWI general Paul von Hindenburg, appointed Hitler chancellor of Germany, as was his right under the Weimar constitution. Hitler thus came to power by legal means, just as his Fascist mentor Mussolini had.

Once in power, Hitler quickly moved to turn Germany into a fascist state. He outlawed other political parties and dispensed with personal freedoms. The SS, the Nazi party police, as well as the Gestapo, the secret police, enforced his totalitarian policies. Hitler also used propaganda and mass rallies to glorify the state and used the Jew as a scapegoat for all Germany's problems. Within weeks of assuming power, Hitler began suspending the rights of Jews. *Kristallnacht* in 1938, "the Night of Broken Glass," reified his policies: Jewish synagogues, businesses, and Jews themselves were attacked during this night of horror. Finally, he

---

4.    Perry, Peden, von Laue, *Sources*, II: 361.
5.    Ibid., 362.
6.    Ibid., 364.

vowed to overturn the Treaty of Versailles. Shortly after assuming power, he told his generals that he would begin to increase the size of the army and that he would build the forbidden aircraft and U-boats; this he began to do, secretly at first, then overtly in 1935.

In 1936 Hitler "tested the waters": he sent the German army into the Rhineland, against the advice of his officers who felt that their army was not yet action-worthy. The Rhineland, you might recollect, was the demilitarized zone stretching along the border between France and Germany and its invasion was a clear violation of the Treaty of Versailles. Despite this, and despite the Locarno Pacts of 1925, no European nation challenged Hitler's actions.

Historians enjoy speculation, the "what ifs" of history. What if Britain, Belgium and France had chosen to confront Hitler at this point? Would he have backed away from his aggressive activities? And, we might ask, why didn't these countries respond to such a flagrantly provocative action?

There were several reasons for their inactivity: many British and French were committed to the idea of pacifism following the carnage of WWI. Many also felt that their governments had dealt too harshly with Germany following the Great War: perhaps Germany did deserve to rearm, to reclaim its land along the Rhineland and to unite with other German peoples. Some Britons believed that the U.S.S.R. posed a greater danger to Western Europe and that a strong Germany in Central Europe was a bulwark against the Communist threat. Finally, the French government had undergone frequent changes; this instability made it difficult for a coherent response to Hitler. The French also relied on their Maginot Line, the system of fortresses that stretched along the German-French border, to safeguard them.

Because of these reasons, Europe allowed Hitler to take over Austria in 1938. After all, many argued, wasn't the *Anschluss,* the union, simply a bringing together of the German peoples, allowing them to fulfill the ideal of national self-determination? When Germany invaded the Sudetenland in 1938, the part of Czechoslovakia bordering Germany, wasn't it again seeking to unite Germans, since three million Germans lived in this area? The rationalization—this appeasement—went on, allowing Hitler to absorb the rest of Czechoslovakia in the spring of 1939.

Meanwhile, in Italy, Mussolini began to act on his belief that a great nation is always an imperialist nation. In 1935, he invaded Ethiopia, one of the last independent kingdoms in Africa, and ruthlessly conquered this country in weeks. The League of Nations condemned Mussolini's actions but did very little to stop him; Hitler, however, endorsed his actions. The Spanish Civil War of 1936–1938, in which Hitler and Mussolini actively supported the Fascist Francisco Franco, ultimately brought these two men together. They solidified their relationship in the Rome-Berlin Axis agreement of 1936, leading to the term "Axis powers" during World War II.

During the 1930s in the Soviet Union, Stalin continued with his totalitarian policies. The secret police worked aggressively to identify "wreckers," those people who supposedly posed threats to the government. Indeed, so intent was Stalin on ferreting out any perceived threats to his control that he executed many of his high-ranking military officers, which hurt the army immeasurably at the outbreak of World War II. He also held a series of "show trials" in which many old Communist loyalists were forced to admit to treasonous crimes and then executed. His reach extended to the everyday folk, and historians estimate that at least 20 million people perished as a result of Stalin's purges.

By the late 1930s, Stalin's focus on fostering "socialism in one country" had reached fruition. He could now turn his attention elsewhere, to those areas which the U.S.S.R. had traditionally controlled. Hitler approached Stalin in the summer of 1939 with the idea of a non-aggression pact, in which each leader pledged to remain neutral should the other go to war. The secret part of this agreement allowed for the division of Poland between Germany and the Soviet Union, and acknowledged Stalin's right to reclaim the Baltic nations. The democracies were shocked that a Communist and Fascist would form such an alliance—and even more shocked when Hitler stormed Poland in September 1939. They had finally had enough. Britain and France declared war on Germany on the third of September: World War II had begun.

## American Isolationism and Pearl Harbor

In the United States the Great Depression was exacerbated by the Dust Bowl, an extreme drought that afflicted the Great Plains, resulting in thousands of impoverished farmers. President Herbert Hoover attempted to deal with these calamities but his policies failed to bring relief. In 1933 Franklin D. Roosevelt (1882–1945) assumed the presidency and initiated "the second American Revolution." FDR, as he is known, implemented a host of new programs to revitalize the American economy. In his New Deal he created programs like the CCC, the Civilian Conservation Corps, and later the WPA, the Works Progress Administration, to put people to work. FDR also introduced Social Security: Americans would no longer need fear the "poor farm" in their old age, nor would the disabled and handicapped have to face extreme poverty. He also attempted to aid the farmers through several plans. Although his programs did make some headway in ameliorating the effects of the Depression, they did not lead to prosperity. It took World War II to achieve that.

In the international arena, America remained isolationist—Europe's issues were not its issues—and Congress passed three neutrality acts, reinforcing this isolationist stance. However, in 1939, in light of Hitler's actions, President Roosevelt pleaded with Congress to reconsider these acts, which it did by allowing a policy of cash-and-carry that would permit the U.S. to sell supplies to Britain and France. Eventually Americans came to see that, as Kansas newspaper editor William Allen White stated, "The future of western civilization is being decided upon the battlefield of Europe."[7] In 1940 Congress increased the defense budget and FDR asked for, and received, the first peacetime draft in United States' history. During this period FDR also met several times with British Prime Minister Churchill to discuss war strategy and philosophy. Indeed, they had determined that when the U.S. ultimately joined the war, 80 percent of its resources would go to defeating Germany first, and 20 percent to vanquishing Japan. With Japan's bombing of Pearl Harbor on December 7, 1941, America ended its isolation and entered the war.

---

7.    Divine, *America Past*, 465.

# 18

## *World War II 1939–1945*

### The War in Europe (1939–1943)

In September 1939, Hitler's *Wehrmacht,* his "war machine," conquered Poland in six weeks through *blitzkrieg*, or "lightening war," tactics: heavy bombing of a site was followed by invasion with tanks, then lighter motorized vehicles, and finally the infantry. Hitler paused during the winter of 1939–1940, then turned his attention to Western Europe. In three brief months, April through early June, Norway, Denmark, the Netherlands, Belgium and France succumbed to Hitler's onslaught. Britain stood alone against the Nazi tyranny.

Britain was alone, yes, but the valiant leadership of Winston Churchill (1883–1965), who had assumed the prime ministership in May 1940, as well as the grit of the British people, made it a formidable foe. Additionally, the British had made good use of new radar technology, positioning stations along the coast to alert them to Luftwaffe incursions. They had also, with the help of some Poles, broken the sophisticated German secret code. And the men of the Royal Air Force, although outnumbered almost two-to-one by the Luftwaffe, rose to the challenge of defending their country. As Churchill said of these men, "Never in the history of a country has so much been owed by so many to so few."

The British bore the brunt of Hitler's wrath for six long months, during the summer and fall of 1940. The Nazis first targeted British airfields and factories, then focused on London, and later cities such as Coventry and Liverpool. Although these air raids would continue throughout the war, and although roughly 40,000 British citizens perished during these attacks, the British never surrendered to the heavy bombardment.

By the spring of 1941, when it became clear that Britain would not succumb to his attacks, Hitler turned his eyes towards the East—remember his idea of *Lebensraum*?—and determined to invade the Soviet Union. It was no matter that he had a non-aggression pact with Stalin; perhaps his attack would take Stalin by surprise, which it did. Before he could attack the U.S.S.R., however, he needed to secure Yugoslavia and Greece. The two months necessary to defeat these countries, April and May of 1941, led to a June invasion of Russia (by one of those strange quirks of history, the same day that Napoleon had begun his ill-fated Russian campaign). But June, as Hitler might have learned from Napoleon, was too late to begin an invasion: winter begins early in the U.S.S.R.

In one major thrust into the U.S.S.R., the Nazis drove to the north, conquered the Baltic countries, then besieged St. Petersburg; they would hold it captive for three long years. Over one million inhabitants died during this period, most from starvation, but the city did not surrender. The German army also pushed towards Moscow, only to be halted by the deep freeze of the Russian winter in late October. The valiant Russian general, Georgi Zhukov, who had organized the defense of St. Petersburg, now launched an offensive from Moscow and drove the Germans from the capital. Zhukov was one of the few high officers who had escaped Stalin's purges, and he continued to lead the Russian armies with energy and determination throughout the war. He should be accorded one of the great heroes of World War II.

In the spring of 1942, Hitler ordered his generals in Russia to initiate a major campaign to the southeast, with the goal of seizing oil-rich territories. During this campaign the Nazis encountered especially fierce resistance at the city of Stalingrad, for Stalin had issued orders that his namesake city should not fall. During the Battle of Stalingrad more than 99 percent of the city was destroyed and over one million Russians perished; nonetheless, the Russians prevailed over the Germans, who lacked adequate supplies and reinforcements, and who suffered thousands of casualties. The surrender of the German army—90,000 troops out of an original 330,000—in February of 1943, made Stalingrad the turning-point battle in Europe. It represented Hitler's first defeat, and the Russians gained offensive momentum from this point on.

While Hitler was waging war against the Allied powers, he was also waging a war of extermination against Jews, gypsies, homosexuals, and other "undesirables," in the name of Aryan supremacy. He began circumscribing the rights of the Jewish people upon assuming power in 1933 with a series of Nuremberg Laws. Later, he ordered his henchmen to initiate round ups, forcing Jews and other targeted groups into labor camps and concentration camps. In 1942, Hitler fixed upon a policy that was called the Final Solution: all the Jews in Europe were to be killed. To accomplish this, the Nazis needed an efficient and cheap method of mass extermination, and Xyclon B, a cyanide-based pesticide, became the product of choice.

The Final Solution worked like this: upon arrival at a concentration camp after a harrowing train trip in which they were packed into cattle cars, those people too ill, too young, or too old to work were separated from the group and herded into an enclosed room, a shower room they were told. The doors were locked, and the room filled with the gas from the poison Xyclon-B pellets. After they were dead, the bodies were removed and incinerated in the ovens of camps such as Chelmo, Auschwitz, and Treblinka. The Nazis killed approximately six million Jewish people during their years in power; those who survived the camps suffered from starvation, torture, beatings, and inhuman medical experiments.

## The War in the Pacific (1931–1945)

Just as Hitler and his Nazis had designs on all of Europe—and possibly the world—Japanese leaders desired control over the Pacific. Although Japan was a democracy headed by the Emperor Hirohito, aggressive military leaders and powerful industrialists seeking overseas materials and markets, influenced Japanese foreign policy. The needs of a burgeoning population also pressured the government into seeking new territorial options. Hence in 1931, Japan attacked Manchuria for its raw materials; reprimanded by the League of Nations for this act of aggression, the Japanese simply withdrew from the League. In 1937, they attacked China, the true beginning of World War II in the Pacific. Then on the 7th of December 1941, Japan launched an attack on the American base at Pearl Harbor, hoping to destroy the American fleet and, ultimately, to gain control of the United States' Pacific territories. The surprise attack on Pearl Harbor, the "day of infamy" as it came to be called, mobilized America into joining the war.

In the first months of the war in the Pacific, Japan enjoyed a series of victories as it swept over the Pacific islands, as well as into Southeast Asia. When Japanese forces attacked the Philippines, American General Douglas MacArthur was ordered to leave his command there, but pledged, "I shall return." Japan captured most of the Allies left in the Philippines and forced them to endure the infamous trek to a prison camp, the Bataan Death March, during which thousands of soldiers perished. Those that survived were held in abysmal conditions for several years until their liberation.

In June 1942, having broken the Japanese code, the Americans prepared to take the Japanese fleet in a surprise attack off the island of Midway. The Battle of Midway is accorded the turning point battle in the Pacific because the Americans destroyed a significant portion of the Japanese fleet and from this point onward took the offensive. Led by Admiral Chester Nimitz in the Central Pacific, the Allies employed a strategy of "island hopping," selecting strategic islands to attack as they moved to the northwest from the Solomon Islands towards Japan. Battles such as Guam, Iwo Jima, and Okinawa were fearsome, for the Japanese ethic of *bushido* meant that a Japanese soldier would fight to the death, making him a tenacious enemy. At Iwo Jima, for example, Americans suffered 30,000 casualties in roughly four weeks of fighting; 18,000 Japanese perished in their effort to retain the island, and just over 1,000 were taken prisoner. Meanwhile, in the Southwest Pacific, troops commanded by General MacArthur retook the Philippines in early 1945, then looked towards Japan.

As the Americans closed in on Japan, the British, too, were on the offensive, moving from their base in India toward their Japanese-occupied colonies of Malaya and Burma. And in China, Mao Zedong and his Communist forces harried the Japanese army during the long years of occupation.

# The North African Campaign

Another key theater of combat was North Africa, where the Italian army, based in Italy's colonies of Libya and Ethiopia, engaged the British army, positioned in Egypt. Mussolini hoped to capture Egypt and gain access to the Suez Canal and the oil-rich lands of the Middle East. The fighting seesawed across Libya and Egypt for two years. However, a major Italian defeat led Hitler to send German troops to support his ally, troops commanded by Erwin Rommel, one of the finest generals of the war. Rommel earned the moniker "the desert fox" because of his stealth and daring in desert warfare. By May 1942, Rommel had enjoyed several victories, had broken through British lines and was closing in on El Alamein, just 200 miles from the Suez Canal. However, in October, Lt. General Bernard Montgomery led a British offensive that drove the Axis forces from El Alamein and back across North Africa into Tunisia. Historians consider the Battle of El Alamein the crucial battle in North Africa; from this point on, the Allies took the offensive.

In early November 1942, American General Dwight D. Eisenhower led his troops into Morocco and Algeria. The Allies planned to trap the Axis army in Tunisia, with the Americans approaching from the west and the British from the east. After some hard-fought engagements, the Allies finally secured North Africa and the Mediterranean.

They then turned their eyes to Italy, just a short distance from North Africa, and in early 1943 launched an invasion in Sicily and southern Italy. As the Allies fought their way up the boot of Italy, they encountered fierce resistance when the Nazis reinforced their Italian allies.

## Other Aspects of World War II

In addition to these major theaters of combat, World War II was waged in other places and in different ways. Aircraft carriers, battleships, and submarines, engaged each other for control of the seas. The war was fought from the air, too, as pilots flew reconnaissance missions and rained bombs on strategic sites, as well as on civilian targets. Airplanes became more sophisticated as the war went on, with jet engines emerging at the war's conclusion. The Nazis also developed the first faster-than-sound missile, the V-2 rocket, and used this weapon against Britain, France and Belgium beginning in late 1944. Spies played a significant role during the war, often utilizing a range of sophisticated espionage tools. Within each country, governments churned out propaganda, demonizing the enemy and inspiring their citizens to contribute to the war effort. In many countries women went to work in factories, school children collected items such as tin foil and bottle caps that could be recycled for wartime use, and families grew their own vegetables in their "victory gardens." Governments also implemented rationing of vital resources, and some mounted campaigns to generate funds for the war chest.

## The Conclusion of World War II

Stalin had increasingly urged Roosevelt and Churchill to mount a major offensive to take pressure off the Soviet Union, which he felt had borne the brunt of the war. Although the Allies had committed some forces to Italy following their success in North Africa, this campaign was not the major European assault that Stalin desired, nor the one that many Allied generals had envisioned. Rather, Supreme Commander of the Allied Forces Dwight D. Eisenhower and his advisors determined that the long-awaited invasion would occur in France, along the beaches of Normandy. A force of three million men, an enormous flotilla of ships, and countless hours of planning went into the operation, which the generals hoped would take place in May 1944. Bad weather prevented the May invasion, and inclement weather again prohibited a June 5th launch. Finally, on June 6th, despite rough seas, the largest land and sea assault in history unfolded as ships ferried troops across the English Channel to land at dawn on the Normandy beaches. During the night, planes dropped paratroopers in the Norman country-side, and gliders carried other combatants across the Channel into France. The Nazis were caught unaware, not expecting an invasion during stormy weather nor along the Normandy coast; however, they quickly regrouped and intense fighting ensued as the Allies made their way from Normandy to Paris, which they reclaimed in late August.

There was one last major European battle—the final gasp of the dying Nazi army—the Battle of the Bulge. This confrontation occurred from December 1944 into January 1945. The Allies finally defeated the Nazis and pushed on toward the Elbe River, where they would shake hands with their comrades-in-arms, the Russians, in May 1945. (Meanwhile, as the Allied armies closed in, Hitler and his mistress Eva Braun had killed themselves in Berlin at the end of April 1945.)

In the Pacific, the Japanese fought on tenaciously. Despite firebomb attacks on Tokyo in which upwards of 100,000 civilians perished, the Japanese refused the Allied demand for an unconditional surrender. Hoping to bring this final theater of war to a conclusion, President Harry S. Truman (who had come to office following Roosevelt's death in April), decided to use the newly developed atomic bomb. This weapon, created under intense secrecy, had been given the code name, "the Manhattan Project." In fact, so secret was this project that Truman, as vice president of the United States, had not been informed of its existence! On August 6th America dropped the first bomb, dubbed "Little Boy," on the city of Hiroshima; three days later it struck Nagasaki with "Fat Man," the second, and last, atomic weapon in its arsenal at the time. On August 14, the Japanese government surrendered—WWII was over.

## A World Changed by War

The results of this war were profound and global. Approximately 60 million people had perished, 20 million of them Russians, six million of them Jews, and many millions of them civilians. Europe lay in ruins, with cities destroyed and economies devastated. Homeless and displaced persons numbered in the millions, with vast numbers of them dying from starvation and exposure after the war.

The political landscape of Europe changed also. As the Soviet Union liberated Eastern Europe from the Nazi tyranny and pushed toward the Elbe River, it became clear to its allies that it had no intention of relinquishing control of these newly freed states. A fresh war, a Cold War, would emerge within a few months, with an "iron curtain" bisecting Germany and eventually placing the Eastern European countries of Hungary, Poland, Rumania, Bulgaria, Albania, and Czechoslovakia under Soviet control. West Germany evolved into a strong and flourishing democracy, while East Germany remained under Soviet hegemony. Berlin, located deep within East Germany, became a divided city, with West Berlin an outpost of West Germany, and East Berlin a part of East Germany. The three Baltic nations, Estonia, Latvia, and Lithuania, created after World War I, were absorbed into the Soviet Union.

Change occurred, too, in the Allied nations. In Britain, Churchill was voted out of office at war's end and Clement Attlee was voted in. Attlee's Labour government passed many pieces of socialist legislation that would grant the British "cradle to grave" economic support. (Churchill was, however, returned to office in 1951.) Charles De Gaulle, self-proclaimed leader of Free France, became the president of the Fourth and Fifth French republics, committed to promoting his nation's influence in the world. In Italy, a series of coalition governments were voted in and out of office, which created political turmoil. And in both France and Italy strong Communist parties emerged for a time following the war, wielding considerable influence in Italy especially. The United States, spared fighting on its soil and possessing the atomic bomb, emerged as a postwar power. Demand for housing and consumer goods fueled its economy, and the postwar period was one of prosperity.

In the Pacific, U.S. forces, led by General MacArthur, occupied Japan from 1945 until 1952. MacArthur worked tirelessly with the Japanese government to promote and instill democracy. Under a constitution that in some ways echoes America's, Japan retained the emperor as a national symbol but established a parliamentary form of government. Men and women aged 20 and over gained the right to vote, and reforms in industry and labor contributed to the growth of democracy. In Article IX of its Constitution, Japan renounced war "as a means of settling international disputes."

The crimes committed during World War II were so heinous that they cried out for justice that would ascribe individual accountability. To that end, the Allied victors created international tribunals in Nuremberg, Germany, in Tokyo, and in other venues to try those deemed most culpable. In establishing these tribunals, the Allies recognized that they were creating a precedent for posterity and strove to clearly identify the crimes.

They determined that engaging in any of the following activities was deserving of punishment: crimes against peace, i.e., perpetrating war; crimes against humanity, i.e. committing atrocities against civilians; war crimes, i.e., violating war conventions in the treatment of soldiers; and conspiracy to engage in any of the above. During the trials every measure was undertaken to represent fairly the accused, and, more time was generally allotted to the defense than to the prosecution. In the case of the Nuremberg Trials, among 22 defendants, three were found innocent, 12 were sentenced to death, and the rest were given prison sentences. (The concept of an International Criminal Court, a world court to try individuals accused of the above crimes, evolved from these tribunals and was realized in 2002; by the end of 2006, more than 100 countries were members of the ICC, as it is called. The U.S. is notably not a member.) Additionally, in 1949, new Geneva Conventions identified and codified war crimes and other breeches of international humanitarian law.

World War II had astonishing effects on Africa and Asia, with strong nationalist movements arising within most African colonies and in Asian colonies such as India, French Indochina, and Indonesia. Natives of these countries, many of whom had fought on behalf of the Allies—on behalf of freedom and democracy—came to believe that they, too, were deserving of independence and personal freedoms. In the British colony of Ghana, Kwame Nkrumah led the first successful African independence movement, agitating against the British; in 1957 it became the first African colony to achieve independence. Inspired by Ghana's success, other Africans clamored for their freedom; gradually the French, Portuguese and Belgians were forced to relinquish control over their colonies, ending the centuries'-long European domination of Africa.

In Asia, too, strong independence movements accelerated after World War II, and most met with success. In India, Mohandas Gandhi had agitated for independence before and during the war; Gandhi's dreams were realized in 1947 when the British allowed India its freedom. In French Indochina, Ho Chi Minh led the Vietminh, a nationalist group determined to oust the French from Vietnam, which it ultimately did in 1954. (As we shall see in the following chapter, Ho's dream of a country controlled by the Vietnamese was not realized until 1975.) The United States granted the Philippines, its sole significant colony, independence in 1946; and in Indonesia, a strong nationalist movement won independence from the Dutch in 1949. Thus ended the great overseas empires.

Additional changes resulted from the war. Politically, women finally gained the vote in countries such as France, Switzerland, Japan, and India. A United Nations was created dedicated to saving "succeeding generations from the scourge of war," as its Preamble avows. The United Nations was modeled on the League of Nations but attempted to rectify the League's shortcomings; as of this writing, over 190 nations hold membership in the UN. Finally, a homeland for the Jews in Palestine, promised by the British in 1917, was realized in 1948 with the formation of the state of Israel. However, the creation of a Jewish state in the midst of a predominately Arab region, and the displacement of over one million Palestinians as a result of the new state, created long-lasting tensions that continue to plague the region—and to polarize the world—today.

## The Arts After World War II

In the 1930s and1940s, European artists had immigrated to America, infusing the art scene with new ideas, energy, and talent. As a result, the United States, and New York City in particular, became the center of the art world. American Jackson Pollock (1912–1956), arguably the most influential painter of the second half of the twentieth century, developed the Action Expressionism movement, hurling paint onto a canvas that was usually placed on the floor. His large and abstract works conveyed the energy and intensity of the artist-at-work. His contemporary, William de Kooning (1904–1997), likewise created bold and energetic abstract works and was a significant contributor to Action Expressionism. Andy Warhol (1928–1987) created "pop art," making multiple pictures of cultural icons such as Marilyn Monroe and of commonplace objects such as Campbell's tomato soup cans. As the century drew to a close, the definition of art greatly expanded: something as mundane as a lipstick tube, or as unusual as a live person sitting in a gallery on display as the *objet d'art,* were considered art.

Composers, too, pushed the boundaries of music following the war. American composer John Cage (1912–1992) wrote experimental pieces in which unusual use was made of traditional instruments and in which some sounds were left to chance. His countryman Philip Glass (1937–) created minimalist pieces; in one of his works, for example, not a single note of music was played! Rock and roll, a unique American form of music, emerged in the early 1950s and was popularized by rock icons such as Elvis Presley (1935–1977). The British were quick to establish their own rock groups, and The Beatles and Rolling Stones gained enormous global influence.

# 19

## *The Cold War*
## *1945–1989*

## East Confronts West: Background to the Cold War

At the conclusion of World War II, the world was plunged into a 45-year Cold War as the U.S. and the U.S.S.R. competed against each other in many different ways and in many different areas. The allies that had jubilantly joined hands at the Elbe River quickly became enemies. Indeed, their underlying philosophies had made them uneasy partners throughout the war: the U.S. espoused democracy, the U.S.S.R was a dictatorship; most Americans embraced Judeo-Christianity, the Soviets were avowedly atheists; the U.S. advocated capitalism, the U.S.S.R. had a state-regulated economy.

The Soviets had their own goals for the postwar world, goals that Americans did not understand or support. Foremost was the desire for security on their western border, the border through which invaders had marched countless times over the centuries. Thus, despite their promises to withdraw their troops from Eastern Europe after the war, they created a system of "satellite" countries there, a buffer zone that would protect them from future invasion. East Germany, Czechoslovakia, Poland, Albania, Bulgaria, and Rumania came under Soviet hegemony, while the Baltic nations were simply absorbed into the U.S.S.R. (Yugoslavia, headed by Josip Tito, became a Communist nation, but one that was independent of Moscow.) The Soviets also desired remuneration for their enormous losses during World War II, losses that far exceeded those of the other Allies. Their satellite nations would provide economic compensation and opportunity for the Soviets; industry was removed wholesale from East Germany, in particular, to help refill Russian coffers. Finally, the Soviets fervently wanted to develop their own atomic arsenal as a defense against America: from their perspective the United States was a potentially dangerous nation, for not only had it created the atomic bomb, but it had also used it!

Of course, from the American perspective the Soviets had abnegated their promise to retreat from Eastern Europe following the war and to promote democracy in the region. The creation of Communist-run satellite states highlighted the duplicitous character of the U.S.S.R. Americans also feared that the Communists, with their professed goal of worldwide revolution, would now actively work to undermine democratic values around the globe. Finally, the U.S. felt a strong distrust of the U.S.S.R. for signing a nonaggression pact with Hitler in 1939—could such a nation be trusted? In light of all of the above, the answer was a resounding "No!"

This new kind of war, a "Cold War," was clearly identified by Winston Churchill in a speech he delivered in Fulton, Missouri in 1946: "From Stettin in the Baltic to Trieste in the Adriatic, an iron curtain has descended across the continent ... Whatever conclusions may be drawn from these facts ... this is certainly not the liberated Europe that we fought to build up."[1] U.S. President Harry Truman responded to the situation by developing the Truman Doctrine in 1947. This policy, while recognizing the "iron curtain" in Europe, asserted that the United States would not permit the spread of communism and, in fact, would actively work to contain it. The Marshall Plan, officially called the European Recovery Act, evolved in late 1947 from the Truman Doctrine. This foreign policy plan gave $12.5 billion dollars to 16 Western European countries. While enormously generous, this huge financial package had a pragmatic goal: to create economically stable European countries in which democracy could flourish. (It is interesting to note that the Marshall Plan also offered aid to the Eastern European nations, which Stalin prevented them from accepting. The Soviets later provided some aid to these countries in a financial package called COMECON.) Under the terms of the Marshall Plan, European countries were encouraged to work together, and in 1952 the European Coal and Steel Community coalesced, dedicated to promoting the growth of heavy industry in six European nations: France, Germany, Italy, Belgium, Luxembourg, and the Netherlands. From this successful organization the Common Market would later emerge, and, ultimately, the European Union. In some respects, it is quite astonishing to see France and Germany join together after centuries of belligerence and acrimony, and so shortly after World War II.

---

1.    Perry, Peden and von Laue, *Sources*, II: 453–454.

# The Cold War Plays Out

As the late 1940s and 1950s unfolded, the U.S. and U.S.S.R. competed against each other in a myriad of ways. Each sought to gain advantage over the other by creating more powerful weapons, and an arms race ensued. When the U.S.S.R. developed the atomic bomb in 1949, President Truman approved the creation of a more powerful nuclear weapon, the hydrogen bomb. The U.S. achieved this by 1952, the Soviet Union in 1953. Each country stockpiled ever more powerful bombs and missiles in a flurry of activity captured by the acronym MAD: mutually assured destruction. The space race was another way in which America and the Soviet Union rivaled each other. In 1957, with the launching of the first satellite, Sputnik, and in 1961 with their orbiting of the first manned satellite, the Soviets seemed to be winning this competition. The U.S. responded by intensifying its space program and by encouraging the study of math and science in schools. It seemingly capped the race by sending the first astronauts to the moon in 1969. Additionally, during this period both the Soviet Union and the United States built a network of spies, and each developed innovative espionage technology, not so different from that showcased in the James Bond films. Berlin, the city where East confronted West most closely, was a focal point for espionage. Finally, even the Olympics became a venue for rivalry: the Soviet Union and its satellite nations, as well as the U.S., worked intensively to develop their athletic programs in order to bring home the gold. Prestige accrued on the world stage to those nations that boasted superior athletes.

During this 45-year period, America and the U.S.S.R. also fought many proxy wars, supporting factions within countries that would further their aims. Most frequently these countries were developing nations and support might be offered through economic packages, armaments, and advisors. In places such as Angola and Egypt, Nicaragua and El Salvador, India and Iran, the Cold War played out to a greater or lesser degree as the two superpowers sought to influence each nation.

In 1962, however, the U.S. and the U.S.S.R. seemed on a collision course over the positioning of nuclear missiles in Cuba, just 90 miles away from the United States. Soviet President Nikita Khrushchev had ordered the placement of nuclear missiles on Cuba, with the acquiescence of Fidel Castro, its Communist leader. When U.S. President John F. Kennedy learned of the missiles, he ordered an embargo on Cuba, allowing no ships access to this island nation. For 13 days in October, Kennedy and Khrushchev played a game of brinksmanship—a game that could have nuclear consequences for the third time in the twentieth century.

Ultimately, Khrushchev "blinked" and ordered the withdrawal of the Russian missiles from Cuba. As a result of this crisis, the U.S. and U.S.S.R. established a hotline, allowing the heads of state instant access to each other to avert future nuclear incidents. Later, the U.S. quietly removed its missiles from West Germany and Turkey, missiles that had the capacity to strike the U.S.S.R.

In two instances during the Cold War, the United States put the Truman Doctrine into action, in Korea and in Vietnam. In 1950 the North Korean army swept across the demilitarized zone at the 38th parallel which separated communist North Korea from (nominally) democratic South Korea. Its goal was to unite Korea under the auspices of communism. The army pushed deep into South Korea, quickly reaching its capital, Seoul. American General Douglas MacArthur, who was guiding the reconstruction of postwar Japan just a short distance away, responded to this aggression by leading American forces into the Korean peninsula. Soon after, he was appointed head of a combined United Nations' force in Korea (although South Koreans and Americans comprised the majority of the UN forces). Fighting was intense for the first year of the conflict, and the North Koreans were aided by 200,000 Chinese troops. Fighting seesawed back and forth across Korea, at great cost to both soldiers and civilians. Jet planes, used extensively for the first time in combat, helped the United Nations' force to prevail, and the conflict ended in 1953. And what was the outcome? Korea was divided into a communist North and democratic South with a demilitarized zone at the 38th parallel—just as it had been at the war's onset.

The situation in Vietnam was somewhat similar to that in Korea. During World War II a strong nationalist group led by the Communist Ho Chi Minh established a regime in northern Vietnam. After the war, the U.S.S.R. and China recognized Ho's rule, while the United States and its allies backed French rule in the south. (Vietnam was part of the French colonial empire.) The French battled Ho's nationalist forces, the Vietminh, for eight years following World War II, but after a terrible defeat at Dien Bien Phu in 1954, they resolved to leave Vietnam. By international agreement the country was divided at the 17th parallel into communist North Vietnam and nominally democratic South Vietnam. At this point the United States began to offer economic support, weapons, and advisors to the pro-American South Vietnamese government. The "domino theory" evolved over this time period: if Vietnam should fall to the Communists, all of Southeast Asia would follow suit—and again, following the tenets of the Truman Doctrine, America would not allow a country or countries to succumb to communism.

Following the Tonkin Gulf Incident of 1964, in which the North Vietnamese allegedly fired on an American ship, President Lyndon Johnson began sending troops to Vietnam, 500,000 of them ultimately. Massive bombing campaigns rained devastation on the country, but despite superiority in weaponry and a large military force, the United States could not prevail without enormous cost against the kind of guerilla war practiced in Vietnam. In this kind of war, it was often difficult to discern friend from foe, for many South Vietnamese, determined to drive out the Americans, joined the Viet Cong, who were allies of the North Vietnamese. The Tet Offensive of 1968, in which the Viet Cong infiltrated major cities in the South, even to the steps of the American embassy in Saigon, began to convince Americans that this war could not be won. In the early 1970s President Richard Nixon began withdrawing troops from Vietnam, and, by 1973, the American forces were gone. During the next two years the North Vietnamese conquered the South and achieved a united Vietnam by 1975.

The Russians, too, faced challenges during the Cold War: in 1956 two of its satellite countries, Hungary and Poland, rebelled against Soviet rule. Moscow responded harshly, making it clear that it would not tolerate any movement towards independence. Twelve years later, in 1968, Czech President Alexander Dubcek called for more freedoms within his country. This movement on behalf of personal liberties, called the Prague Spring, was eventually crushed when Soviet President Leonid Brezhnev ordered in troops and tanks. Just as President Truman had espoused the policy of "containment" 20 years earlier, Brezhnev vowed, in a twist on this idea, that no communist country would be allowed to break away from Marxist-Leninist ideals.

The Brezhnev Doctrine was tested in 1979 when Afghan rebels—called the *mujahideen*—threatened to topple the Soviet-backed government of Afghanistan. Brezhnev, still the president of the U.S.S.R., committed Soviet troops to support the government. Ten years of guerilla warfare ensued, with the *mujahideen* ferociously opposing the Russian forces. (The United States armed the Afghan rebels with weapons, among which was a group known as the Taliban.) With each passing year Russian casualties mounted, and the war grew increasingly unpopular in the U.S.S.R. Finally, in 1989, Soviet President Mikhail Gorbachev ordered the troops home.

# The End of the Cold War: Gorbachev and the Collapse of the Soviet Empire

With the advent of Mikhail Gorbachev (1931–), the Cold War began to thaw. Gorbachev, who assumed the presidency of the U.S.S.R. in 1985, was a new kind of Soviet leader, one who called for domestic policies of *glasnost*—openness—and *perestroika*—a restructuring of the economic and political systems. These policies allowed for more personal freedoms, multiple political parties, and some private economic development. He also encouraged the leaders of the satellite nations to allow similar freedoms and declared, "Each people determines the future of its own country and chooses its own form of society. There must be no interference from outside, no matter what the pretext."[2] Additionally, American President Ronald Reagan (1911–2004) applied much pressure on the Soviets to curtail their repressive activities.

Heartened by Gorbachev's words, in 1989 Lech Walesa and his Solidarity party led the Poles to independence, toppling the Communist regime and calling for free elections. Hungary, East Germany, Czechoslovakia and Rumania followed suit; this time, there was no objection from the Kremlin, and in each of these countries general elections followed the *coups*. The toppling of the Berlin Wall in the autumn of 1989 remains a cogent symbol of the downfall of communism in Eastern Europe: with its destruction, East Berliners and West Berliners walked freely into each other's arms for the first time in almost 30 years.

Meanwhile, within the U.S.S.R., the myriad of ethnic peoples was restive: should each of them not have their independence, too? Beginning in 1990, Lithuania sought to gain its freedom from the U.S.S.R. Although Gorbachev had allowed the satellites to break free from the orbit of the U.S.S.R., he did not want Lithuania, an integral part of the U.S.S.R., to do so. He feared that if Lithuania achieved its independence, other Soviet republics would follow its example. He ordered troops to quell the drive for freedom, an action condemned at home and abroad, and that spurred the republics to demand their independence.

In 1991 the flamboyant and powerful former mayor of Moscow, Boris Yeltsin (1931–2007), was elected president of the Russian republic. He openly criticized Gorbachev's policies and inspired the Soviet republics to seize their freedom—which they did. By December 1991, the Soviet Union had dissolved and Gorbachev was without a job. Some of the 15 newly formed states united into

---

2.    Beck, *Modern World History*, 542.

the CIS, the Commonwealth of Independent States, over which Russia, as the largest and most powerful of these states, has much influence.

# The New Republics

Since the dissolution of the U.S.S.R. some of its former republics, like the Baltic nations, have embraced democracy, while a few like Ukraine have lurched toward it. Others, such as Turkmenistan and Uzbekistan, have become dictatorships along the lines of the old Soviet model. In Russia, President Vladimir Putin (1952–) has led his nation since the resignation of President Yeltsin on December 31, 1999. While Putin maintains that Russia is a democracy, over the years he has exercised censorship over the media, nationalized some privately owned companies, and consolidated his power. Despite its diminished status post-Cold War, Putin's policies have made clear his intent for Russia to play a major role in the world.

Another communist country, Yugoslavia, slowly dissolved following the death of strongman Josip Tito in 1980. Tito had kept in check the incendiary mix of Serbs, Croats, Slovenes, Muslims, Christians, and others living within Yugoslavia, a federation of six republics. In the early 1990s, and again in the late 1990s, war broke out in some of these republics when the Serbs sought to impose their leadership. Fighting in Bosnia was especially cruel, with Bosnian Serbs employing a policy of "ethnic cleansing"—torture, rape, and murder—to eradicate the Muslim population. By 1999, however, with NATO involvement, the independent republics of Slovenia, Croatia, Bosnia and Herzegovina, Macedonia, and Serbia had emerged. The Yugoslav region of Kosovo, filled with ethnic Albanians, has recently declared its independence from Serbia.

# 20

## *The West Today: Some Final Thoughts*

At the end of the Cold War, the United States emerged as the world's lone super-power. Its mighty arsenal and strong economy gave it great global influence; its promise of economic opportunity and personal freedoms drew immigrants from around the world; its energetic people, among the hardest working in the world, continued to invent and create, contributing to major breakthroughs in technology, medicine, and science.

Yet with this leadership role has come great responsibility—a responsibility that critics contend the U.S. has shirked by not signing the Kyoto Protocol, which established environmental regulations, and by refusing to join the International Criminal Court. Critics assert, too, that the United States has arrogantly ignored world opinion to pursue its own course, thereby alienating many of its traditional allies. Only time will tell if, what is now called "the United States' empire" will decline in the 21$^{st}$ century—as we have seen, all empires eventually do.

And what of Europe, the birthplace of ideas and events that shaped Western civilization? Many European countries today are wrestling with issues of high unemployment, declining native populations, stagnant economies, and increasing numbers of immigrants. While problems such as these confront nations like Britain, Germany, and France, they, nonetheless, have retained leadership roles in the world.

The dream of a federation of European states, the European Union, was realized in 1993. The EU, as of this writing, unites 27 nations—over 480 million people—under its auspices and has the potential to wield considerable economic and political clout. However, this union lacks popular support in many countries where nationalism continues to trump the notion of union.

Indeed, nationalism, or in many cases what we might call ethnic loyalty, continues to be a major force in the West, uniting and dividing peoples. East and West Germany united into a greater Germany in 1990 at the end of the Cold War, while Czechoslovakia divided into the Czech Republic and Slovakia in 1993. After a decade of bitter ethnic fighting in the 1990s, Yugoslavia divided into several states. In Russia, the people of Chechnya have continued to demand their independence, as have the Basques in Spain.

At the dawn of the 21$^{st}$ century, we must wonder about the future role of the West, which has given the world powerful ideas about freedom, toleration, and opportunity; of respect for the individual; of legal equality and justice; and of pride in one's country. The West, with its discoveries and inventions that have led to a deeper understanding of the physical world, greater material comfort, and vastly improved health. The West, which has also led the globe into cruel wars and that has controlled and exploited many of the world's peoples.

While we do not know the future of the West, or even if the term and all it represents will have relevance in another century, we do know that we live in an interconnected world, much more so than at any time in history. We know that environmental concerns, burgeoning populations, global terrorism, deadly pandemics, nuclear proliferation—these and other issues affect all of us. We know, too, that there will be opportunity for rising nations like China and India to make major contributions to the destiny of our planet.

Despite the host of issues confronting the world today, this writer holds fast to the words of Enlightenment philosopher Marquis de Condorcet in her hopes for the future: "Nature has set no term to the perfection of human faculties ... the progress of the perfectibility ... will doubtless vary in speed, but it will never be reversed as long as the earth occupies its present place in the system of the universe...."[1]

---

1.    Perry, Peden and von Laue, *Sources*, II: 94.

# Bibliography

Beck, Roger, et al. *Modern World History: Patterns of Interaction.* Evanston: McDougal Littell, 2001.

Billson, Charles J. *The Aeneid of Virgil.* New York: Dover Publications, 1995.

Brower, Reuben A., Anne D. Ferry, and David Kalstone. *Beginning with Poems: An Anthology.* New York: W.W. Norton & Co., Inc., 1966.

Brown, Thomas, ed. *American Eras: 1850–1870. Civil War and Reconstruction.* Detroit: Gale, 1997.

Chambers, Mortimer, et al. *The Western Experience,* 6th ed. New York: McGraw-Hill, Inc., 1995, Vol. I.

Cotterell, Arthur, ed. *The Encyclopedia of Ancient Civilizations.* London: Penguin Books, 1980.

Divine, Robert A., et al. *America Past and Present.* Brief 3rd ed. NY: Harper Collins College Publishers, 1994.

Eisen, Sydney and Maurice Filler. *The Human Adventure: Readings in World History.* New York: Harcourt Brace Jovanovich, 1964, Vol. I.

Eisen, Sydney and Maurice Filler. *The Human Adventure: Readings in World History.* New York: Harcourt Brace Jovanovich, 1964, Vol. II.

Esler, Anthony. *The Western World: Prehistory to the Present.* Englewood Cliffs, New Jersey: Prentice Hall, 1994.

Finley, John H. Jr. *The Complete Writings of Thucycidides: The Peloponnesian War.* New York: The Modern Library, 1951.

Flory, Harriet and Samuel Jenike. *The Modern World: 16th Century to the Present.* White Plains, N.Y.: Longman Press, 1992.

Hefner, Richard D. *A Documentary History of the United States: An Expanded Edition*. New York: The New American Library, 1963.

Howarth, Tony. *Twentieth Century History: The World Since 1900*. 2nd ed., Josh Brooman. New York: Longman, Inc., 1989.

Howe, Helen and Robert T. Howe. *Ancient and Medieval Worlds*. White Plains, NY: Longman Inc., 1987.

*In the Footsteps of Alexander the Great*. Dir. David Wallace. Perf. Michael Wood. Distributor: PBS Home Video, 1997.

McKay, John, Bennett D. Hill, and John Buckler. *A History of Western Society*. Boston: Houghton Mifflin Company, 1995, Vol. II.

Nagle, D. Brendan. *The Ancient World: A Social and Cultural History*. 5th ed. Upper Saddle River, NJ: Prentice Hall, 1999.

Nevins, Allan and Henry Steele Commager. *A Pocket History of the United States*. New York: Washington Square Press, 1981.

Palmer, R.R., Joel Colton, and Lloyd Kramer. *A History of the Modern World*. 9th ed. New York: Alfred A. Knopf, 2002.

Perry, Marvin, Joseph R. Peden, and Theodore H. Von Laue. *Sources of the Western Tradition*. 2nd ed. Boston: Houghton Mifflin, 1991, Vol.1.

Perry, Marvin, Joseph R. Peden, and Theodore H. Von Laue. *Sources of the Western Tradition*. 5th ed. Boston: Houghton Mifflin, 2003, Vol. II.

Scarre, Christopher and Brian M. Fagan. *Ancient Civilizations*. New York: Longman, 1997.

Strayer, Joseph R. and Dana C. Munro. *The Middle Ages, 395–1500*. 4th ed. New York: Appleton-Century-Crofts, Inc., 1956.

Ward, Geoffrey C., Ken Burns, and Ric Burns. *The Civil War: An Illustrated History*. New York: Alfred A. Knopf, 1990.

Willson, David Harris. *A History of England*. New York: Holt, Rinehart and Winston, Inc., 1967.

978-0-595-47047-1
0-595-47047-5

Made in the USA
Las Vegas, NV
09 December 2021

36865567R00100